Detail from a fresco at Viansa Winery and Italian Marketplace by Evans and Brown: At Viansa, as in Tuscany, wine and food are an integral part of the good life.

Jerry and Marita
Merry Christmas from
my Cucina to yours!
Vicki Sebastiani
Dec. 1996

Cucina Viansa

VIANSA WINERY AND ITALIAN MARKETPLACE

A collection of recipes from
Viansa Winery by

VICKI SEBASTIANI

"CUCINA VIANSA"
by Vicki Sebastiani
Viansa Winery and Italian Marketplace
25200 Arnold Drive
Sonoma, California 95476

First Edition
Printed in the United States of America

10 9 8 7 6 5 4 3 2 1
ISBN: 0-9654979-3-3

To purchase additional copies,
please write, call or fax:
Viansa Winery and Italian Marketplace
25200 Arnold Drive
Sonoma, California 95476
1-800-995-4740 or
FAX 707-935-4731

ACKNOWLEDGEMENTS

Book Designer: Patti Britton, Britton Design
Editor: Penny Popken
Photographer: Joyce Oudkerk Pool
Photographer of Front Winery Photo and Back Cover: M.J. Wickham
Food Stylist: Bunny Martin
Calligrapher: Georgia Deaver
Word processor: Adrianne Fellows-Hanson
Typesetting/Production: Patty Holden
My Personal Assistant: Kristina Torres

Special thanks to
my husband, Sam—my inspiration and sustenance

our children, Lisa, Moira, Joe, Jonathan, Michael, Liz and Chris—willing recipients of recipe testing

and my mother, Irene Annabel Koster, for being there for me all these years.

CONTENUTO

Table of Contents

Introduzione

Introduction

Since the day Vicki and I met, I felt there was a special connection between us.
But the first time she cooked dinner for me, I was surprised to find a tremendous added bonus.
During my three decades in the wine business, I have dined throughout the United States and Europe.
I have broken bread with dignitaries and enjoyed countless meals prepared by famous chefs.
Yet rarely has a meal come close to rivaling our family dinners, simple but sublime menus created by Vicki,
combining the best techniques and ingredients from California and Tuscany.
My tribute to my wife's cooking is unqualified:
She is truly a great cook.

The village church in the tiny town of Farneta contains detailed records of the lives of generations of Sebastianis.

In our home, as in Tuscany, the kitchen is the heart of family life.

Each evening as we gather for dinner, our kitchen table is transformed into an island of calm in a sea of chaos. It is here that we laugh together, cry together and share our hopes and dreams with each other. Most importantly, it is here that we gather together for simple meals, for holidays and birthdays, to celebrate the food and wine that are so much a part of Viansa.

When Sam and I first dreamed of creating Viansa more than a decade ago, we envisioned it as a special place where we could expand our family to include visitors who could learn about wine and food in a friendly atmosphere. Sam has concentrated on creating an array of fine wines from both California and Italian grapes. I have focused my efforts on preparing delicious foods to complement his exciting results.

Just as every wine you taste at Viansa has Sam's imprint, every food you sample reflects my style. From the Cal-Ital™ creations in the delis at both Viansa and Lo Spuntino to the pantry foods for sale in the marketplace and the meals served at Viansa's special events, all were born or refined in my kitchen.

Many of these creations are adaptations of family favorites, others are my interpretations of Tuscan specialties our family has enjoyed during trips to Italy. Some are spur-of-the-moment solutions to an overabundance of ripe, seasonal produce, and some are last-minute creations dreamed up when unexpected company arrived at the door.

Over the years, Viansa customers have cajoled me to share my recipes, and I have done so for the last few years through our Tuscan Club, Viansa's monthly food and wine club. But that wasn't enough; customers and staff insisted that I write a cookbook.

And so "Cucina Viansa" was born.

Through this book, I hope to share with you my love of good food—both Tuscan and Californian—regardless of your culinary background. I firmly believe that one needn't attend culinary school in order to cook well, and my recipes reflect this belief.

Each recipe is basic enough for the novice cook, yet exciting enough for the advanced cook. Ingredients, though fresh and flavorful, are easy to locate, whether you live in San Francisco, Santa Fe or Savannah.

Most importantly, I hope that "Cucina Viansa" enables you to recreate a bit of the Viansa experience in your own home. You may not be able to savor my creations seated under an olive tree overlooking the Viansa wetlands, but you'll be able to enjoy the many flavors that are so much a part of the Viansa dream!

Cuciniamo! Vicki

Dedication

To my husband, Sam,

my partner in exploring the bounty of the Tuscan table

and to our children,

with whom we share our love

of the cuisine of our heritage.

Antipasti

Appetizers

At Viansa we savor every part of the Tuscan meal,

beginning with the antipasti—the savory nibbles that serve to whet the appetite.

Crisp bruschetta laden with vine-ripened tomatoes and basil,

creamy brie with roasted garlic, savory frittatas—

delicious choices to begin a meal.

The peasants of Farneta return home from a fruitful day in the fields.

SALSA DI POMODORO FRESCO "CAL-ITAL"

Cal-Ital™ Fresh Garden Salsa

The widespread and ever-increasing popularity of salsa convinced me to create an Italian version from the bounty of Viansa's garden. Use your imagination and customize it with your favorite flavors. If you love really hot salsa, leave the seeds in the chile pepper. We love this salsa as a veggie and/or chip dip, on top of scrambled eggs and slightly drained and combined with cottage cheese.

4 medium vine-ripened tomatoes

1 small red onion, minced

½ fresh red chile pepper, seeded and minced

3 cloves garlic, minced

2 tablespoons minced Italian parsley

¼ red bell pepper, minced

12 leaves fresh basil, minced

2 tablespoons minced chives

Seed three of the tomatoes and chop into small pieces. Seed the remaining tomato and purée in a blender or food processor. Combine the remaining ingredients with the chopped and puréed tomatoes.

Chill for at least 1 hour to combine flavors. Serve with unsalted tortilla chips.

Makes 4 cups.

NOTE: To use as a vegetable dip, seed and finely chop all four tomatoes. Combine with remaining ingredients and add ¼ cup Viansa Sun-Dried Tomato Aioli and 2 cups drained cottage cheese.

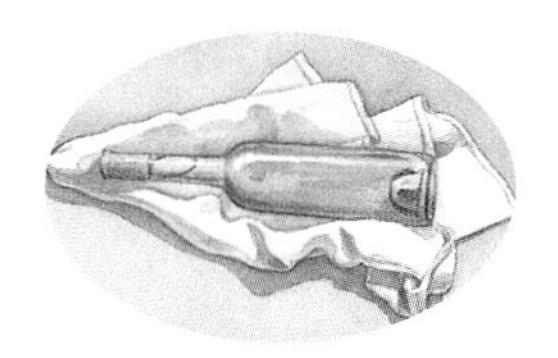

VIANSA WINE SUGGESTION
'Imbianco' Barbera Rosé or 'Augusto' Barbera

FUNGHI ARROSTITI CON PESTO

Pesto-Stuffed Mushroom Caps

PESTO SAUCE

1 cup Viansa Extra Virgin Olive Oil

½ cup chopped walnuts

2 tablespoons pine nuts

3 cups fresh basil leaves

6 cloves garlic

1 cup chopped fresh spinach, plunged in boiling water for 2 to 3 minutes and squeezed dry

1 cup freshly grated Parmesan cheese

Salt and freshly ground pepper to taste

24 large mushrooms, approximately 1½-inches in diameter

OPTIONAL

24 rolled anchovies, canned snails, or fresh or canned mussels

Preheat oven to 500°F.

Combine ½ cup of the olive oil with the walnuts, pine nuts, basil, garlic, spinach, cheese, salt and pepper in a food processor or blender and purée until smooth. With motor running, slowly drizzle in the remaining olive oil, blending well.

Remove stems from mushrooms and clean the caps, reserving stems for another use. If desired, place anchovy, snail or mussel in the mushroom cavity. Spoon 1 heaping teaspoon of the pesto mixture into each mushroom cap. Place mushrooms in a shallow baking pan.

Bake 7 to 10 minutes, until mushrooms are browned and the pesto sauce is bubbling. Serve hot.

Makes 24 servings.

The best way to clean mushrooms is with a soft vegetable brush. Any loose soil comes off easily and the mushrooms retain their earthy freshness without getting soggy. A soft toothbrush also works fine. If desired, substitute Viansa Red Pepper Pesto, Yellow Pepper Pesto or Olive Anchovy Pesto for the Pesto Sauce in this recipe.

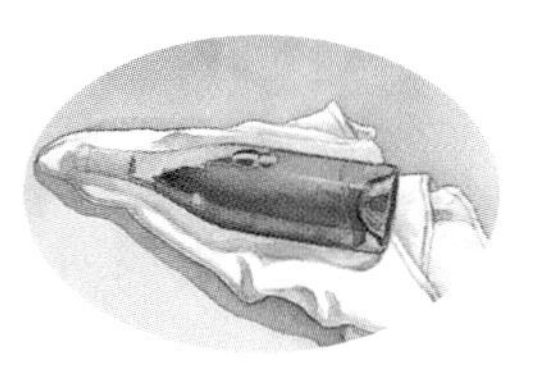

VIANSA WINE SUGGESTION

Chardonnay, 'Vittoria' Pinot Grigio or Nebbiolo

Mussels Florentine, Goat Cheese and Roasted Pepper Tart, and Bruschetta

COZZE ALLA FIORENTINA

Mussels Florentine

3 dozen mussels

¼ cup minced shallots (2 to 3 large shallots)

1¼ cups dry white wine

¼ cup freshly squeezed lemon juice

1 cup (2 sticks) unsalted butter, cut into tablespoon size pieces

1 bunch fresh spinach

OPTIONAL
Thin strips of red pepper for garnish

In a large, heavy saucepan, bring 1 cup water to a boil. Wash mussel shells and add to boiling water. Cover and cook until mussels open. Discard any mussels that have not opened. Drain the mussels and let cool enough to handle. Pull them out of the shells and snip off the "beard" with a pair of scissors. Set mussels aside and keep warm. Discard half of the shells and reserve the others.

Clean the spinach, trim off any large stems and plunge into a fresh pot of boiling water for 3 to 4 minutes. Drain well. When cool enough to handle, chop spinach coarsely. Keep warm.

In a small skillet, combine shallots, wine and lemon juice. Reduce over low heat until liquid is nearly gone (watch carefully as the reduction will scorch easily at this point). Remove pan from heat and add one or two pieces of butter. Stir steadily with a whisk until the butter is no longer in a solid form, yet not liquid either. It should resemble the consistency of a thin mayonnaise. Incorporate the rest of the butter, one or two pieces at a time, returning the pan to a low heat as necessary, retaining the same consistency. If butter separates, the heat is too high; remove it from the heat and whisk rapidly to re-emulsify. Set sauce aside and cover to keep warm.

To serve, place about 1 teaspoon of the warm spinach in each reserved half shell and top with a warm mussel. Pour 2 teaspoons warm sauce over each. If desired, garnish with slivers of red pepper. Serve immediately.

Makes 36 servings.

The freshest mussels are those that are still tightly closed when you purchase them. If fresh mussels are unavailable, substitute fresh clams or oysters in the shell. You could also use any frozen shellfish and place them in purchased scallop shells (available at import stores). If all else fails, use toast triangles.

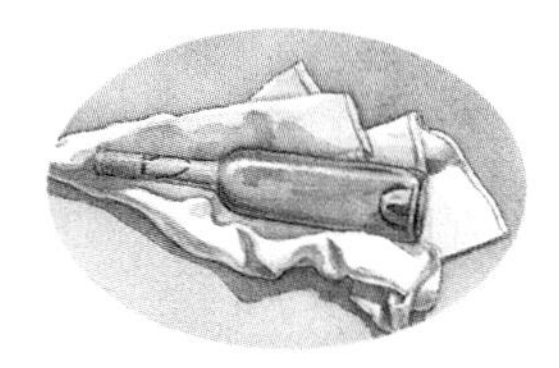

VIANSA WINE SUGGESTION
Sauvignon Blanc or Nebbiolo

CROSTATA DI CAPRINO E PEPERONI ROSSI

Goat Cheese and Roasted Pepper Tart with Basil-Chive Crust

Roasting peppers is a simple procedure that yields delicious results: sweet peppers that are a versatile cooking ingredient. You can roast the peppers under the broiler, but if you have a gas range it is quicker to char the peppers over the flame. Or char extra peppers on your grill the next time you fire it up.

This tart looks terrific prepared in a quiche or tart pan with a removable side ring that exposes the "ruffled" crust. Another suggestion would be to prepare it in smaller tartlet pans for individual servings.

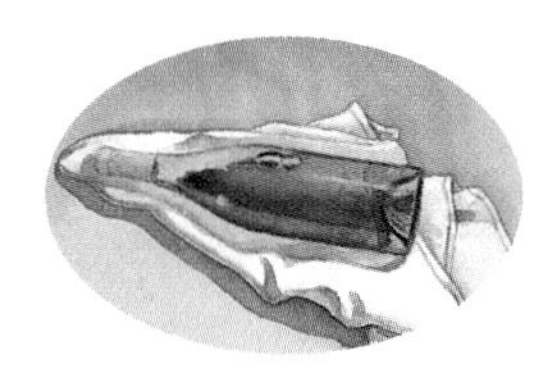

VIANSA WINE SUGGESTION'
'Riserva Anatra Bianco' Trebbiano, 'Imbianco' Barbera Rosé or 'Athena' Dolcetto

CRUST

1 cup all-purpose flour

2 tablespoons powdered sugar

½ cup cold unsalted butter (1 stick), cut into small pieces

2 teaspoons minced fresh basil

1 teaspoon minced fresh chives

FILLING

2 red bell peppers

1 cup (about 10 ounces) fresh goat cheese

½ cup half-and-half or milk

2 tablespoons dry white wine

3 eggs

4 ounces lean prosciutto, chopped or sliced into small pieces (Canadian bacon may be substituted)

CRUST

Combine flour, sugar, butter and herbs in a food processor and process until the dough forms a large ball (or mix dough using your usual pie crust method). Press dough to about ⅛-inch thickness on the bottom and up the sides of a 9-inch fluted tart, quiche or pie pan with sides ¾ to 1-inch high. Set aside.

FILLING

Roast the peppers over a flame (or under the broiler) until charred on all sides. Place in a closed paper bag for 15 minutes to steam, and then peel off the skin, cut in half and discard membranes and seeds. Coarsely chop one pepper, and cut the other into long, thin strips.

Preheat oven to 375°F.

Purée the goat cheese, half-and-half, wine and eggs until smooth. Add prosciutto and chopped pepper, mixing well. Pour the filling into the crust and decorate the top with the strips of roasted pepper. Bake 45 to 50 minutes, just until mixture has set and the top has slightly browned.

Serves 12 (it is somewhat rich, so I serve small slices).

(See photograph on page 12.)

BRUSCHETTA POMODORO

Garlic Toast with Chopped Tomatoes and Herbs

BRUSCHETTA

16 to 18 slices sourdough baguettes, each about ½-inch thick

5 cloves garlic, peeled and sliced into thirds, lengthwise

½ cup Viansa Extra Virgin Olive Oil

POMODORO TOPPING

¼ cup Viansa Extra Virgin Olive Oil

2 cloves garlic, minced

1 tablespoon Viansa Cabernet Wine Vinegar

Salt and pepper to taste

3 large Roma tomatoes (about ½ pound), seeded and diced

¼ cup diced red onion

10 to 12 kalamata olives, pitted and chopped

12 large basil leaves, finely chopped

BRUSCHETTA

Toast baguette slices on both sides under broiler until lightly browned. Rub one side of toasted bread with cut side of garlic and brush with olive oil. Top with Pomodoro Topping, or open your refrigerator door or cupboard and get creative with different toppings!

Makes 16 to 18 slices.

POMODORO TOPPING

Combine oil and garlic in a large bowl, and let stand for at least one hour. Add vinegar, salt and pepper and whisk until emulsified. Add tomatoes, red onion, olives and basil and toss with the vinaigrette. If possible, cover and set aside at room temperature for a couple of hours, tossing occasionally, to allow the flavors to marry before serving.

To serve, top bruschetta toasts with about 2 tablespoons of tomato mixture.

(See photograph on page 12.)

Once you try bruschetta, you are sure to love it! Bruschetta is the original Italian garlic bread and it combines a trio of healthful and delicious foods: grains, olive oil and garlic. The very best flavor comes from toasting the bread over hardwood coals. However, if this is not possible, you can use a broiler. I find the easiest method is to simply toast large slices of bread in the toaster until a very light brown, then cut them into halves or quarters.

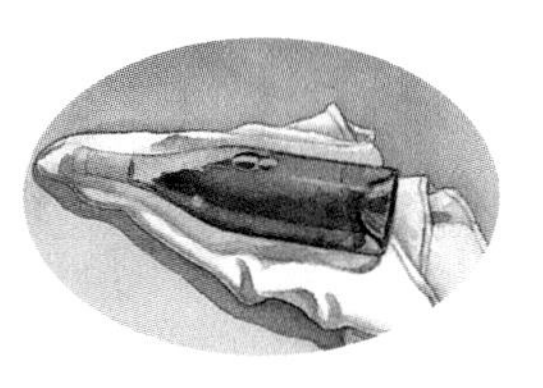

VIANSA WINE SUGGESTION

Chardonnay or 'Piccolo Toscano' Sangiovese

BRUSCHETTA CON OSTRICHE AL PESTO

Garlic Toast with Oysters and Pesto

Grated Parmesan cheese is now available in the fresh cheese section of many supermarkets and cheese shops. Due to the high cost of authentic Parmigiano Reggiano, these grated cheeses are usually a blend of several other cheeses in addition to the Parmesan. Using a blend is OK if the cheese is going to be combined with strong flavors, such as the basil and garlic in this pesto. However, if grating Parmesan on top of a finished dish, freshly grated Parmigiano Reggiano is a must!

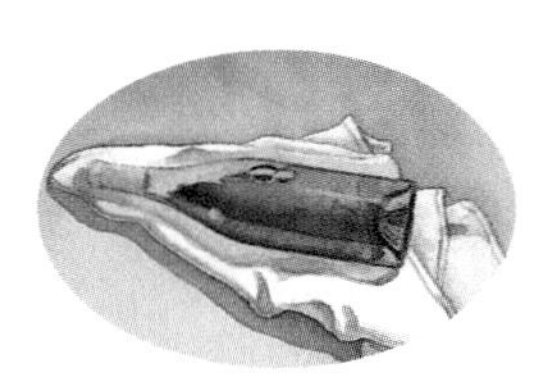

VIANSA WINE SUGGESTION

Reserve Chardonnay or 'Riserva Anatra Rosso' Cabernet Sauvignon

PESTO

½ cup Viansa Extra Virgin Olive Oil

2 tablespoons chopped walnuts

1 tablespoon pine nuts

1½ cups fresh basil leaves, loosely packed

2 tablespoons minced fresh oregano leaves

2 tablespoons minced Italian parsley

3 cloves garlic

½ cup freshly grated Parmesan cheese

⅛ teaspoon freshly ground black pepper

OYSTERS

2 jars (10 ounces each) fresh oysters

Approximately ¾ cup flour

½ cup butter (1 stick)

6 slices ½-inch thick sourdough bread

PESTO

Combine all of the Pesto ingredients in a food processor or blender and purée until smooth. Set aside.

Makes 1 cup pesto.

OYSTERS

Rinse the oysters in cold water. Drain well and pat dry. (If the oysters are large, cut them in half. If they are very small, put two on each toast.) Dredge oysters in flour, shaking off excess. In a large skillet, melt the butter and sauté the oysters over medium heat until light brown.

Meanwhile, trim the crusts off the bread and lightly toast the slices. Cut the toast diagonally into triangle shapes and place in a plastic bag to keep warm.

To assemble, carefully warm the pesto (this can be done ahead by partially placing a small bowl of pesto into a larger bowl of very hot water; do not warm it in a saucepan over heat, as it browns very easily). To serve, place a hot oyster on each toast triangle and top with a tablespoon of warm pesto.

Makes approximately 12 bruschetta.

BAGNA ALL'AGLIO

Garlic and Herb Dipping Oil

⅔ cup Viansa Extra Virgin Olive Oil

¼ cup Viansa Balsamic Vinegar

5 large cloves garlic, minced

1 tablespoon minced fresh thyme leaves

1 tablespoon minced fresh rosemary

½ teaspoon crushed red pepper

1 teaspoon freshly ground black pepper

Mix all the ingredients to combine, but don't blend to the point of emulsifying. (I usually put the ingredients in a jar and shake well.) The taste improves if made a day in advance. Store in refrigerator, but bring to room temperature to serve.

Makes 1 cup.

NOTE: Once chopped and placed in olive oil, the fresh herbs and garlic are perishable. The dipping oil should be used within two weeks of preparation. To extend the shelf life of olive oil and keep it fresh tasting, store it in a cool, dark place.

It is as customary to have olive oil on every Italian table as it is to have salt and pepper on American tables. We include a decanter of Viansa's Extra Virgin Olive Oil on every table at our wedding and corporate dinners for guests to enjoy with our wonderful foccacia bread.

Many Italian restaurants have taken the traditional oil one step further, adding garlic and fresh herbs. Just be sure you have a good supply of bread on hand when you put this zesty oil on the table! If you want to recreate a Viansa experience, serve this dipping oil with my Foccacia Bread recipe on page 113.

Brie with Roasted Garlic

FORMAGGIO ALL'AGLIO ARROSTITO

Brie with Roasted Garlic

1 cup garlic cloves (about 5 heads)

½ cup olive oil

1 large wheel Brie cheese (about 2 pounds) or 3 small wheels Brie (8 ounces each)

½ cup kalamata olives, pitted and cut into halves or quarters

1 tablespoon minced Italian parsley

Immerse peeled garlic cloves in boiling water for 3 minutes. Drain and pat dry. In a small, heavy saucepan or skillet, cook the garlic cloves in oil over medium-high heat for about 7 minutes, turning continuously until golden brown. Remove garlic cloves from oil and drain on paper towels. Cool garlic oil and reserve for other uses such as sautéing vegetables or chicken.

Preheat oven to 400°F.

Carefully slice the thin rind off the top of the Brie wheel. Place wheel on a baking sheet, cut side up. With a small sharp knife, slice the garlic cloves diagonally, being careful not to completely sever the slices. Gently press garlic cloves into fans. Arrange garlic fans and olive pieces decoratively on the top of the Brie.

Bake, uncovered, for 8 to 9 minutes or until Brie is warm and slightly softened. Remove from the oven and sprinkle the warm Brie with minced parsley. Carefully transfer to a serving plate and serve with crackers, apple wedges or bread.

NOTE: Baking the Brie to melt it slightly is optional. If you choose to serve it this way, be sure to melt it just before serving so that it is warm and soft.

Makes 15 to 20 servings.

We use so much roasted garlic in Viansa and Lo Spuntino dishes that I developed a speedy method of blanching and sautéing the garlic to obtain the same sweet, delicious results as baking the whole heads. Cooked garlic cloves keep well in the refrigerator, so make a large batch to have "roasted" garlic available when needed.

Many markets sell garlic cloves already peeled in plastic containers of varying sizes. One cup of raw, peeled garlic contains about 74 cloves. One head of garlic contains about 14 cloves.

The olive oil remaining from pan-roasting the garlic is terrific in salad dressings, for bread dipping, or for sautéing vegetables or chicken.

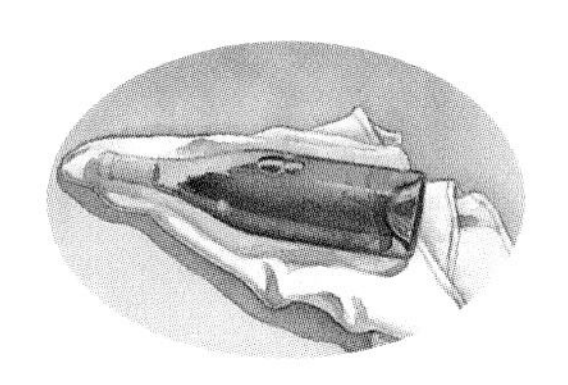

VIANSA WINE SUGGESTION

'Cento per Cento' Chardonnay or 'Thalia' Sangiovese

CROSTINI CON POMODORI SECCHI E CAPRINO

Sun-Dried Tomato and Goat Cheese Crostini

I always keep a supply of crostini on hand. It is a great way to use up leftover bread. Crostini can accompany soup or salads, or they can be spread with a topping of your choice. Crostini can be made ahead of time and stored in an airtight plastic bag at room temperature for up to 2 weeks or frozen until needed.

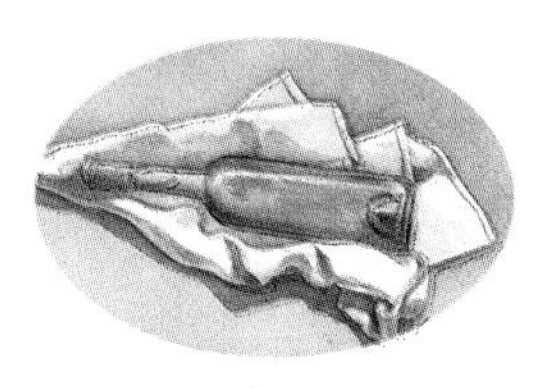

VIANSA WINE SUGGESTION
'Vittoria' Pinot Grigio, Sauvignon Blanc or 'Imbianco' Barbera Rosé

CROSTINI

1 sourdough baguette (about ½ pound)

8 cloves garlic, minced

½ cup olive oil

2 tablespoons dried Italian seasoning

SUN-DRIED TOMATO GOAT CHEESE

8 ounces fresh goat cheese, at room temperature

⅔ cup Viansa Sun-Dried Tomato Pesto

CROSTINI

Preheat oven to 375°F.

Cut baguette into 48 slices (each ¼-inch to ½-inch thick) and place in a large bowl. Combine minced garlic with olive oil. Drizzle garlic oil over bread slices very slowly, tossing frequently to coat all slices as evenly as possible. Sprinkle Italian seasoning, one tablespoon at a time, evenly over oiled bread slices, tossing frequently. Place seasoned slices on a baking sheet in a single layer. Bake for 10 to 12 minutes, until golden brown.

SUN-DRIED TOMATO GOAT CHEESE

Purée the goat cheese and pesto in a food processor, or mix well with a fork.

To serve crostini, spread two teaspoons goat cheese mixture onto each crostini slice. If you want a fancier presentation, you can use a pastry bag with a large decorative tip. If you like, garnish crostini with a slice of sun-dried tomato, a slice of black olive, a leaf of Italian parsley or some minced chives.

Makes approximately 48 crostini, depending on size of baguette.

CROSTINI CON FAGIOLI E GAMBERETTI

Shrimp with White Bean and Chive Purée on Crostini

CROSTINI

1 sourdough baguette (about ½ pound)

8 cloves garlic, minced

½ cup olive oil

2 tablespoons dried Italian seasoning

TOPPING

1 bunch (at least ½ ounce) chives

1 can (15 ounces) cannellini beans (white kidney beans), well drained

½ cup minced yellow bell pepper

2 cloves garlic, minced

½ teaspoon salt

Pinch white pepper

⅓ cup mascarpone cheese (cream cheese may be substituted)

½ pound large cooked bay shrimp (about 2 cups)

CROSTINI

Preheat oven to 375°F.

Cut baguette into 48 slices (each ¼-inch to ½-inch thick) and place in a large bowl. Combine minced garlic with olive oil. Drizzle garlic oil over bread slices very slowly, tossing frequently to coat all slices as evenly as possible. Sprinkle Italian seasoning, one tablespoon at a time, evenly over oiled bread slices, tossing frequently. Place seasoned slices on a baking sheet in a single layer. Bake for 10 to 12 minutes, until golden brown.

TOPPING

Mince enough of the chives to equal 3 tablespoons. Reserve remaining chive stems for garnish.

Place beans, bell pepper, minced chives and garlic into a food processor or blender. Purée for 1 to 2 minutes, until mixture has a thick, creamy consistency. Add salt, pepper and cheese, and purée until the cheese is incorporated into the mixture.

Spoon a heaping teaspoonful onto each crostini and top with shrimp. (If the largest shrimp you are able to purchase seem small, top with 2 shrimp. The recommended ½ pound of shrimp will provide an adequate amount.)

To garnish, cut the remaining chive stems into 48 1-inch pieces and tuck one piece into white bean puree, next to the shrimp.

Makes approximately 48 crostini, depending on size of baguette.

Unlike bruschetta, which is toasted bread rubbed with garlic and drizzled with olive oil, crostini is usually fried and then spread with toppings. I developed this oven-baked version which has terrific flavors, but much less oil. The crunchy little toasts are adaptable to almost any hors d'oeuvre spread.

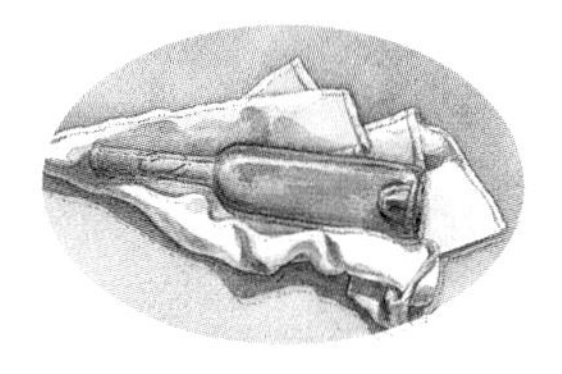

VIANSA WINE SUGGESTION

'Imbianco' Barbera Rosé, Chardonnay or 'Di Pacomio' Aleatico

Pepper and Prosciutto Frittata

FRITTATA DI PEPERONI E PROSCIUTTO

Pepper and Prosciutto Frittata

6 large eggs

¼ cup slivered prosciutto

2 tablespoons chopped roasted red peppers

⅓ cup coarsely chopped fresh spinach

1 teaspoon honey

¼ teaspoon salt

2 tablespoons freshly grated Parmesan cheese

2 tablespoons Viansa Extra Virgin Olive Oil

In a medium bowl, beat eggs with a fork or whisk. Stir in the remaining ingredients, except the olive oil.

Heat a 9 to 10-inch skillet or omelet pan over medium heat and add olive oil. When it is hot enough to make the eggs sizzle, add the egg mixture. Immediately reduce the heat to low and cook over gentle heat, uncovered, until the frittata is set but not browned, about 12 to 15 minutes. (The egg mixture in the center of the skillet will lose its liquid appearance when set. Take care not to overcook the eggs or they will lose their delicacy.) To finish cooking, slide the pan under a preheated broiler, 6 inches from the heat, for 1 to 2 minutes, until the top is golden. Use a spatula to loosen the edges and slide the frittata onto a serving plate.

Serve warm or cold, cut into wedges.

Serves 4.

Frittata panini—frittata sandwiches—are very popular throughout Tuscany. You will even find them sold at gas stations! For a delicious panino of your own, place frittata slices on fresh bread spread with one of Viansa's pestos or mustards.

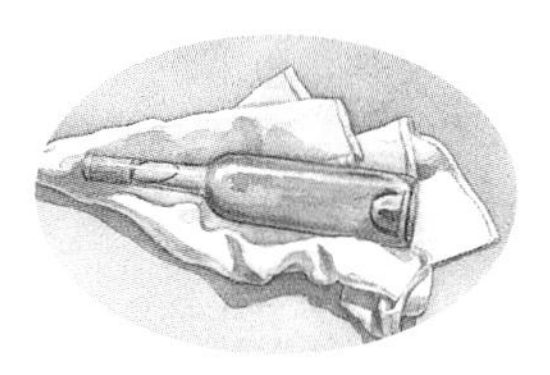

VIANSA WINE SUGGESTION

Sauvignon Blanc or 'Piccolo Toscano' Sangiovese

FRITTATA DI FORMAGGIO E PEPERONCINI

Cheese and Chile Frittata

Frittata is loosely defined as an Italian omelet. Actually, it is a colloquialism for the Italian expression "fare una frittata" (to make a mess). Frittatas consist of beaten eggs combined with various cooked vegetables, meats, herbs or cheese and can be cooked on the stove or baked in the oven.

In this recipe I combine common California ingredients in an Italian frittata—my Cal-Ital™ concept—and change this usually flat frittata into a thicker baked dish that can be served hot or cold at a picnic, a buffet, as an appetizer, side dish or as a main dish at brunch.

VIANSA WINE SUGGESTION
'Augusto' Barbera or
Well chilled 'Imbianco' Barbera Rosé

2½ cups grated Jack cheese (½ pound)

2½ cups grated sharp cheddar cheese (½ pound)

2 cans (4 ounces each) diced green chiles, drained

1 can (13-ounces) evaporated milk

⅓ cup flour

4 eggs, beaten

½ teaspoon salt

In a 9x13-inch shallow baking dish, layer half the Jack cheese and half the cheddar cheese. Spread chiles over the cheese and top with the remaining half of the cheddar and Jack cheeses. Recipe can be prepared one day ahead to this point. Cover and keep refrigerated.

Preheat oven to 350°F.

Mix about ½ cup evaporated milk with flour and stir to make a thin paste, dissolving any lumps. In a medium bowl, add the milk and flour paste to the remaining evaporated milk, eggs, and salt. Whisk well to thoroughly combine and pour over cheese.

Bake for approximately 40 minutes, until frittata is a very light golden brown on top. Baked frittata can be served hot, at room temperature or cold.

Makes 24 squares, approximately 2 inches each.

SFOGLIA CON LUMACHE AL PESTO

Escargot Pesto Puffs

15 cloves garlic

1 cup Italian parsley leaves, loosely packed

1 cup fresh basil leaves, loosely packed

3 tablespoons olive oil

Pinch of salt and pepper

1 can (7 ounces) large or giant snails (about 1 dozen snails)

1 sheet puff pastry (available in the supermarket frozen food section; each 1 pound-1¼ ounce box contains two unbaked puff pastry sheets)

1 egg, beaten

1 tablespoon water

Combine the garlic, parsley, basil, oil, salt and pepper in a food processor or blender and purée.

Rinse snails in cold water, drain well and cut in half.

Preheat oven to 350°F.

Thaw one sheet of frozen puff pastry according to package directions. Mix egg and 1 tablespoon water in a small bowl. On a lightly floured surface, roll the sheet of pastry out to 15x15-inches, and cut into 3-inch squares. Place ½ teaspoon of herb pesto and ½ snail on each square. Brush egg and water mixture on the edges of the square and pinch together to seal (you could fold the edges over to make triangles if you prefer). Place on an ungreased baking sheet and brush each top with egg mixture. (The Escargot Pesto Puffs can be made ahead of time and refrigerated until ready to bake.)

Bake for 15 to 18 minutes, or until lightly browned. Serve hot.

Makes 25 servings.

Italians have been enjoying snails in their cuisine for centuries. Many of their numerous holidays include a snail dish of one type or another. Americans are much more squeamish and appear to enjoy them in French escargot fashion, with lots of garlic, parsley and butter. This version is sure to be loved by all!

This herb pesto is a modification of my favorite basil pesto. Since you'll probably purchase the Italian parsley and basil by the bunch, you could make more of the herb mixture than this recipe calls for and toss it with pasta! The herb pesto will keep in a jar in the refrigerator for weeks.

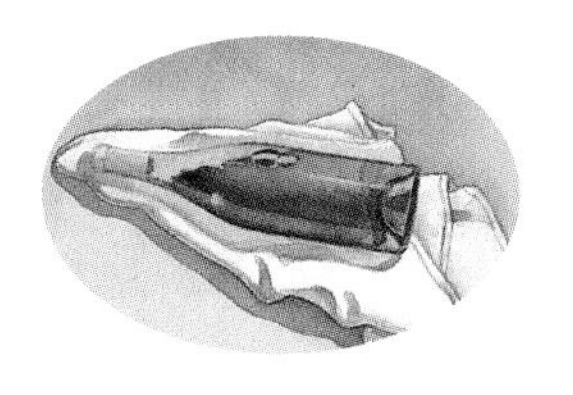

VIANSA WINE SUGGESTION

'Cento per Cento' Chardonnay or Reserve Cabernet Sauvignon

FRITTELLE ALLA FRUTTA CON ANATRA AFFUMICATA

Cranberry-Orange Griddle Cakes with Smoked Duck

When grating citrus zest, be sure to grate only the colored portion of the rind, called the zest. The white pith underneath the zest is quite bitter.

We are very fortunate in Sonoma to have a wonderful duck farm owned and operated by a local family. One of their specialties is a moist and succulent smoked duck breast. If desired, substitute a sliver of meat of your choice. Top griddle cakes with a dollop of Viansa Peperoni Rossi Saporiti, our luscious Red Pepper Relish, for additional color and flavor.

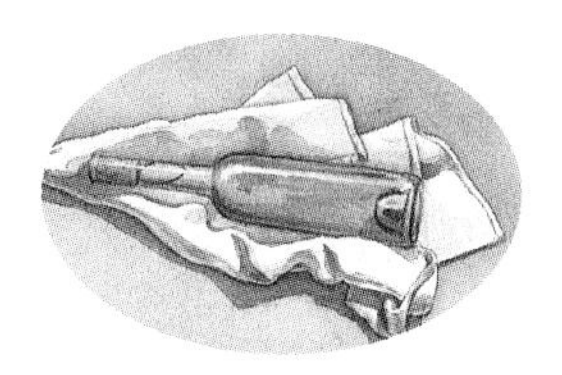

VIANSA WINE SUGGESTION
'Vittoria' Pinot Grigio, Sauvignon Blanc or 'Di Pacomio' Aleatico

¼ cup dry white wine

½ cup sweetened dried cranberries (about 2½ ounces)

1 cup flour

2 teaspoons baking powder

¼ teaspoon salt

5 teaspoons sugar

1 egg, well beaten

¾ cup milk

1 tablespoon finely grated orange zest

10 ounces smoked duck, ham or cured meat of your choice

3 tablespoons sour cream

Heat wine and soak cranberries in it for 10 to 15 minutes; set aside.

Combine the flour, baking powder, salt and sugar, and mix well. Combine the beaten egg with milk, orange zest, cranberries and wine. Add the liquid mixture to the flour mixture and beat until smooth.

Heat a large non-stick skillet until hot. Using a tablespoon, spoon batter into hot skillet, forming mini-cakes about 1 inch in diameter. Cook on both sides until golden. Be sure each spoonful contains a cranberry or two, as they tend to sink to the bottom of the batter. Remove to a baking rack to cool, or to a warm serving platter if serving warm.

Cut the meat into 36 slices (about ¼ ounce each). Dab each piece of meat with about ¼ teaspoon of sour cream and "glue" it onto a griddle cake. Serve warm or at room temperature.

If desired, top with additional tiny dollop of sour cream and a sliver of chive or minced chives to garnish.

Makes 36 cakes.

ROTOLO DI POLLO

Rolled Chicken with Fresh Herbs, Spinach and Cheese

FILLING

1 tablespoon minced fresh basil

1 tablespoon minced fresh rosemary

1 tablespoon minced fresh thyme

2 packages (10 ounces each) frozen chopped spinach, thawed and squeezed dry

½ cup ricotta cheese

½ cup grated Asiago cheese

½ teaspoon salt

¼ teaspoon pepper

1 small yellow onion, minced

4 cloves garlic, minced

1 tablespoon olive oil

CHICKEN

8 boneless and skinless chicken breasts (about 6 ounces each)

⅓ cup Viansa Hot Sweet Mustard

1 roasted red bell pepper, sliced into 16 strips

1 tablespoon olive oil

1 tablespoon fresh thyme leaves

¼ cup white wine

FILLING

In a medium bowl, combine the basil, rosemary, thyme, spinach, ricotta and Asiago cheeses and salt and pepper. In a medium sauté pan, sauté onion and garlic in olive oil until translucent, about 8 to 10 minutes. Remove from heat and mix into the herb and cheese mixture.

Preheat oven to 350°F.

CHICKEN

With a kitchen hammer or heavy flat object such as a wine bottle, gently pound each breast to flatten to about ¼-inch thickness. Brush each breast with about 2 teaspoons mustard. Carefully spread about ¼ cup of the spinach mixture on each flattened breast. Place 2 slices of roasted pepper along the center and carefully roll up each breast as tightly as possible without the filling oozing out. Place seam side down in a lightly oiled shallow baking dish, about 9x13-inches. Brush the chicken rolls with olive oil and sprinkle with 1 tablespoon thyme leaves. Pour the white wine in the bottom of the baking dish, cover with aluminum foil and bake for 10 minutes. Remove foil and bake for another 15 minutes. Remove chicken rolls from oven and cool about 15 minutes before slicing. Slice into ½-inch thick slices and serve hot or cold.

Makes about 64 hors d'oeuvres.

Serves 8 as an entree.

We have served this versatile chicken recipe as both hot and cold hors d'oeuvres, as a luncheon or picnic dish, or even as an informal dinner entree.

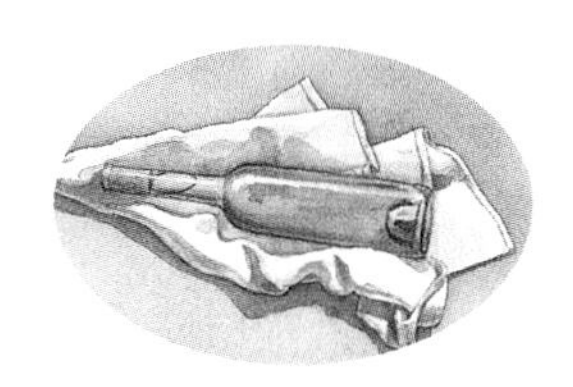

VIANSA WINE SUGGESTION

Sauvignon Blanc or Nebbiolo

Pasta, Riso, Polenta e Gnocchi

Pasta, Rice, Polenta and Gnocchi

From humble beginnings such as wheat, rice, corn meal and potato
come some of Tuscany's finest dishes—savory pastas,
creamy risotto, satisfying polenta, and tender dumplings of gnocchi.
In this chapter I share with you Italian classics, family favorites
and Viansa specialties.

The walled city of Lucca was the center of commerce for the villagers from tiny Farneta.

RADIATORE AL POLLO

Radiatore Pasta with Grilled Chicken, Bocconcini and Roasted Garlic

This grilled chicken pasta with tender chunks of fresh mozzarella, piquant olives and creamy roasted garlic is one of the most popular pasta dishes in our Marketplace.

If desired, substitute baked chicken for the grilled chicken, penne pasta for the radiatore and use your own sauce. If you don't have any Viansa Sun-Dried Tomato Pesto and you cannot locate a substitute, use half the Marinara Sauce recipe found on page 34 (Cannelloni recipe). Substitute it for both the pesto and marinara sauce in this recipe.

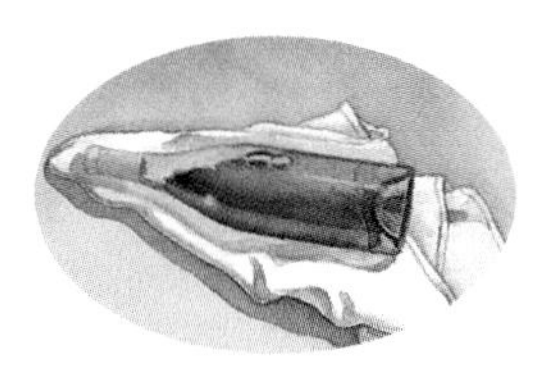

VIANSA WINE SUGGESTION
Chardonnay or
'Thalia' Sangiovese

ROASTED GARLIC

1 cup garlic cloves (about 5 heads garlic)

½ cup olive oil

PASTA

1 teaspoon salt

1 tablespoon olive oil

1 pound radiatore or penne pasta

6 chicken breasts (about 8 ounces each), grilled and cut into bite-size chunks

2 cups Viansa Sun-Dried Tomato Pesto (see sidebar)

1 cup marinara or red pasta sauce (see sidebar)

2 cups fresh basil leaves, julienned (sliced into ribbons)

1 cup kalamata olives, pitted and halved

2 packages (8 ounces each) bocconcini, cut in half (bocconcini are small fresh mozzarella balls packed in water, sold in the refrigerated cheese section of many markets)

Bring a small pan of water to boil. Immerse garlic cloves in boiling water for three minutes. Drain and pat dry. In a small, heavy saucepan or skillet, heat the olive oil and cook the garlic cloves over medium-high heat for about 7 minutes, turning continuously, until golden brown. Remove garlic cloves from oil and drain on paper towels. Cool garlic oil and reserve for other uses such as salad dressings or sautéing vegetables or chicken.

Bring 4 quarts water to a boil in a large, deep pot. Add salt, oil and pasta and cook until al dente (barely tender). Drain pasta and return to the large pot. Add the remaining ingredients and toss to combine. Add roasted garlic and toss again.

To serve, heat the pasta over low heat just until bocconcini begin to melt.

Serves 8 as a main course, 10 to 12 as an appetizer.

PASTA AI PEPERONI CON SEMI DI ZUCCA

Six-Pepper Pasta with Pumpkin Seeds

¼ cup shelled raw pumpkin seeds (about 2½ ounces)

2 yellow bell peppers

1 red bell pepper

2 Anaheim, pasilla or poblano chiles

¼ cup olive oil

2 cloves garlic, minced

½ cup marinated Italian peperoncini (about 8 large peperoncini), stemmed, seeded and minced

⅛ to ¼ teaspoon cayenne pepper, depending on taste

⅛ teaspoon ground white pepper

½ teaspoon salt

1 pound tri-colored fusilli pasta

Toast pumpkin seeds on a baking sheet in a 325°F oven for 5 to 7 minutes, until they swell and start popping. Remove from oven and allow to cool.

Remove the core, membrane and seeds from peppers and chiles and cut into matchstick-size pieces. Heat a large skillet over medium-high heat. Add oil, peppers and chiles. Sauté for 10 to 12 minutes, until limp. Add garlic, peperoncini, cayenne, white pepper and salt. Stir to combine, cooking another 2 to 3 minutes.

Meanwhile, cook the pasta in a large pot of boiling salted water until al dente (barely tender). Drain pasta, return to pot and add pepper mixture. If serving hot, add toasted pumpkin seeds and toss over medium heat. If serving cold, remove from heat, stir in seeds and chill.

Serves 8 as an appetizer, 4 as a light entree.

If you are a fan of hot flavors, here is your recipe! To turn up the temperature in this California-Italian pepper pasta, increase the Anaheim chile and peperoncini as much as you want, and use more of their seeds. Be careful with the cayenne and taste as you add—the fresher the pepper, the hotter it will be!

VIANSA WINE SUGGESTION
'Augusto' Barbera or 'Riserva Anatra Bianco' Trebbiano

Fettuccine with Clams, Squid and Spicy Sauce

PASTA SOFFRITO AI FRUTTI DI MARE

Fettuccine with Clams, Squid and Spicy Sauce

SOFFRITO SAUCE

2 slices bacon, minced

2 tablespoons olive oil

1 medium yellow onion, minced

1 large stalk celery, minced

2 cloves garlic, minced

¼ cup chopped Italian parsley

1 large carrot, peeled and minced

½ teaspoon salt

¼ teaspoon pepper

1 can (28 ounces) peeled Italian plum tomatoes, drained

½ cup red wine

2 tablespoons seeded and minced marinated Italian peperoncini (about 2 large peperoncini)

FETTUCCINE

½ pound dry fettuccine

1 tablespoon olive oil

CLAMS AND SQUID

1½ pounds calamari (squid)

16 fresh clams (in the shell)

SOFFRITO SAUCE

In a medium skillet, cook the bacon until crisp. Add the oil, onion, celery, garlic, parsley and carrot. Add salt and pepper to taste. Sauté 3 to 4 minutes, or until vegetables are wilted.

Add the tomatoes and mash with a fork or spoon. Add the wine and simmer, uncovered, for approximately 20 minutes, until the sauce thickens. Stir in the peperoncini and simmer for another 2 to 3 minutes. Makes 3 cups sauce.

FETTUCCINE

Cook pasta in a large pot of boiling salted water until al dente. Drain, toss with olive oil and return to pot to keep warm.

CLAMS AND SQUID

To clean calamari, cut the tentacle portion from the body by cutting below the eyes. Squeeze out the mouth portion (which looks like a garbanzo bean) and discard. Remove the remaining head portion from the body and discard along with the insides from the squid's body, being sure to pull out the transparent cartilage (its backbone). Although the skin is edible, you can remove the thin purple skin from the body by scraping or peeling it off, if desired. Rinse tentacles and bodies under cold running water. Cut squid bodies into 1-inch rings.

Bring one quart water to a boil in a medium-large saucepan and immerse calamari bodies and tentacles. Reduce heat and simmer approximately 1 to 2 minutes, until bodies are no longer translucent and the edges of the rings begin to curl. Remove immediately and keep warm, retaining cooking liquid.

To clean clams, scrub shells under cold running water with a vegetable brush. Immerse clams in the calamari water, boiling gently, until shells pop open. Remove clams from water and keep warm. Discard any clams that do not open.

To serve, arrange hot fettuccine on a warm serving dish and top with hot calamari, clams and soffrito sauce.

Serves 8.

Soffrito is the classic base sauce used for many pasta and meat dishes in Italian cuisine. It always contains minced onion, celery and carrot. It usually includes garlic and parsley, and it sometimes includes meat. I have chosen to use them all, and I think you'll agree the results are delicious!

Calamari, or squid, is a favorite Tuscan seafood. It has a mild, sweet flavor and a pleasantly firm texture. Either fresh or frozen squid is fine. The squid in most markets has been flash frozen, then thawed and sold as "fresh". The difference between flash frozen and truly fresh calamari is almost imperceptible.

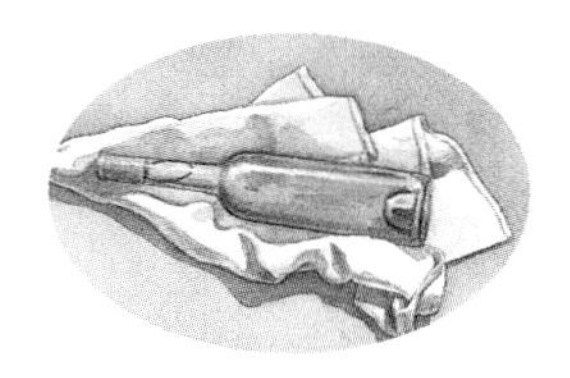

VIANSA WINE SUGGESTION

Sauvignon Blanc or Nebbiolo

CANNELLONI DI FORMAGGIO E ERBE CON SALSA MARINARA

Cheese and Herb Cannelloni with Marinara Sauce

Although "alla marinara" sauce is usually associated with seafood dishes, meaning simply "in the sailor's style," I find this simple sauce of tomatoes, olive oil, wine and fresh herbs is perfect with my cheese cannelloni.

If desired, substitute dried manicotti or cannelloni shells purchased at your market. Making the crepes yourself takes a little more time, but I'm sure you'll agree that the freshly made crepes are divine and defy comparison to any dried substitute! Crepes can be prepared ahead and refrigerated for a day or so if necessary.

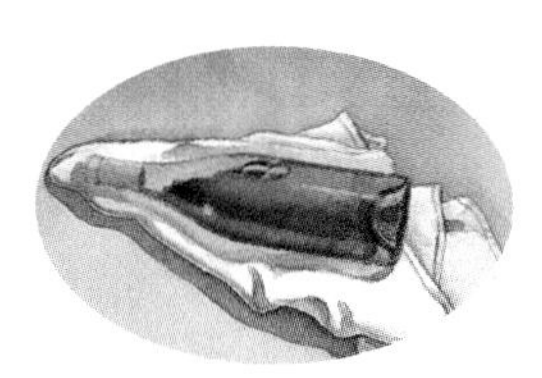

VIANSA WINE SUGGESTION

Chardonnay or Nebbiolo

CREPES

2 large eggs
1 teaspoon salt
1 tablespoon sugar
¼ cup chilled white wine
¾ cup flour
1¼ cups milk
olive oil

FILLING

2 cups ricotta cheese
¾ cup freshly grated Parmesan cheese
2 packages (8 ounces each) cream cheese, at room temperature
2 eggs, slightly beaten
½ cup minced green onions, including green tops
2 tablespoons minced Italian parsley
2 tablespoons minced fresh basil
¼ teaspoon salt
Dash pepper

MARINARA SAUCE

¼ cup olive oil
4 cloves garlic, minced
2 medium yellow onions, chopped
2 cans (28 ounces each) Italian plum tomatoes
½ cup red wine
1 teaspoon minced fresh oregano
1 teaspoon minced fresh basil
½ teaspoon salt
¼ teaspoon pepper
¾ cup freshly grated Parmesan cheese

CREPES

In a medium bowl, whisk eggs until frothy. Add salt, sugar and wine and whisk thoroughly. Add flour and milk alternately, beating well after each addition. Cover and allow the batter to rest one hour in the refrigerator. Whisk again to mix.

Spread a very small amount of olive oil with a brush (or paper towel) on a 6 to 8-inch non-stick crepe pan or skillet. Pour 3 tablespoons batter into the skillet for each crepe (use a large cooking or serving spoon that holds three tablespoons, so you can pour the batter all at once). Quickly swirl to spread the batter to a 6-inch circle. Brown lightly on the underside over medium heat, turn to briefly brown the second side (use a rubber spatula to loosen the crepe around the edges, slide it under and flip the crepe over). Slide each crepe onto waxed paper. Crepes can be stacked between layers of waxed paper until ready for use. If preparing well ahead of time, wrap the stack of crepes in plastic wrap and refrigerate.

Makes 12 to 14 crepes.

FILLING

Combine the ricotta, grated Parmesan, cream cheese and eggs in an electric mixer or food processor and mix until well blended. Add the remaining filling ingredients and mix to combine. Spread about ⅓ cup of filling down the center of each crepe. Fold the sides of the crepe over the filling to form a roll. Place filled crepes, seam side down, in a single layer in a shallow 9x13-inch baking dish.

MARINARA SAUCE

Preheat oven to 350°F.

Heat oil in a large skillet and sauté garlic and onions for 10 to 12 minutes, until tender. Drain 1 cup of the liquid from the canned tomatoes and discard or save for another use. Stir the tomatoes (mashing with a fork or spoon to incorporate), remaining tomato liquid, wine, oregano, basil, salt and pepper into the onions. Bring to a boil, reduce heat and simmer 20 minutes, stirring occasionally. Pour the Marinara Sauce over the cannelloni and sprinkle the Parmesan over the top. Bake for 40 minutes. Makes 6 cups sauce.

Serves 6 (2 crepes each).

GNOCCHI DI ZUCCA

Pumpkin Gnocchi

1½ pounds fresh pumpkin, butternut or banana squash (skin and seeds removed)

1½ cups flour

3 tablespoons melted butter

Pinch of salt

Pinch of white pepper

Pinch of nutmeg

¼ cup melted butter

½ cup freshly grated Parmesan cheese

2 tablespoons minced Italian parsley

Preheat oven to 300°F.

Cut pumpkin into small pieces and steam until barely tender. Don't overcook. Drain and place in oven for 7 to 8 minutes in order to remove excess moisture. Purée the dry pumpkin in a food processor or blender, or pass through a strainer. Allow to cool completely. Stir the flour, 3 tablespoons melted butter, salt, pepper and nutmeg into the cooled pumpkin.

On a lightly floured surface, roll the dough with your hands into logs about ¾-inch in diameter. Cut the logs into 1-inch pieces, handling the dough carefully, as it is fairly soft. If it seems too sticky, add more flour until it is easy to handle. (To prepare gnocchi in advance, simply transfer the logs of uncooked gnocchi to a plate and wrap tightly with plastic wrap. Slice into smaller pieces just before cooking.)

Cook the gnocchi in a large pot of rapidly boiling water until they float to the surface. Remove with a slotted spoon or wire skimmer and drain. Toss with ¼ cup melted butter, then with grated Parmesan. Sprinkle with minced parsley just before serving. Cooked gnocchi can be refrigerated, with or without the butter and cheese coating, and reheated in a 300°F oven for 7 to 8 minutes.

Makes approximately 48 to 50 gnocchi, enough for 4 to 6 servings.

This recipe produces a light, loosely-shaped gnocchi. It is very suitable for a meal you want to prepare in advance, as it can be refrigerated at almost any point of preparation and completed later on. Serve Pumpkin Gnocchi as a first course, a light entree or a side dish. It is delicious served plain, or topped with a carrot sauce or a nut-flavored cream sauce.

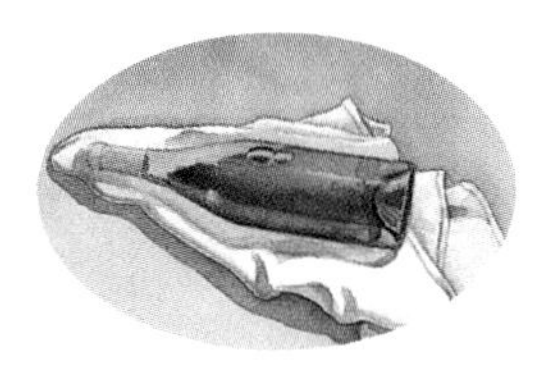

VIANSA WINE SUGGESTION
Reserve Chardonnay or Nebbiolo

Rolled Vegetable and Cheese Pasta

ROTOLO DI PASTA CON VERDURE E FORMAGGIO

Rolled Vegetable and Cheese Pasta

2 tablespoons butter

1 cup finely diced fennel (1 small bulb)

1 cup finely diced leek (1 large leek)

3 cloves garlic, minced

1 tablespoon dried fennel seed, slightly crushed

½ teaspoon salt

¼ teaspoon pepper

⅓ cup dry white wine

2 packages (10 ounces each) frozen chopped spinach, thawed and squeezed dry

¾ cup chopped roasted red peppers

1 cup ricotta cheese

¼ cup freshly grated Parmesan cheese

¼ cup freshly grated Asiago cheese

1 sheet (9x20-inches) thin, fresh pasta (about ½ pound)

2¼ cups marinara or red pasta sauce (see sidebar)

Melt butter in a large skillet and sauté fennel, leek, garlic and fennel seed over medium heat for about 15 minutes, until vegetables are limp. Season with salt and pepper, add wine, reduce heat slightly and continue cooking an additional 12 to 15 minutes, until liquid has evaporated. Set aside to cool for about 15 minutes.

Mix together the spinach, roasted peppers, ricotta and grated cheeses and add to the cooled fennel mixture.

Preheat oven to 350°F.

Lay out the pasta sheet and brush with ½ cup marinara sauce. Spread the filling mixture evenly over pasta, covering to within ½-inch of all the edges. Carefully roll up the pasta and filling lengthwise so the resulting roll is about 9 inches long and 4 inches wide. Spread ½ cup of marinara sauce on the bottom of a shallow baking dish. Carefully transfer the pasta roll to the baking dish and spread another ½ cup sauce on the top. Cover loosely with foil and bake 1 hour.

Remove the pasta roll from the oven and allow it to cool 15 to 20 minutes before serving. To serve, remove foil, carefully cut pasta roll into ¾-inch thick slices and place on a serving platter. Top each slice with a tablespoon or two of warm marinara sauce, or pass sauce at the table.

VARIATION: SUBSTITUTE DRIED LASAGNA NOODLES FOR PASTA SHEET: Cook 12 wide (not extra wide) lasagna noodles according to package directions until tender. Drain. Spread ⅓ cup filling along the length of each noodle and roll up. Spread ¾ cup marinara sauce in the bottom of a shallow baking dish (about 8x8-inches). Stand the lasagna roll-ups on end in the baking dish and top with 1½ cups sauce. Sprinkle top with additional grated Asiago cheese, cover loosely with foil and bake 1 hour.

Serves 6 to 8.

Pasta Rotolo is a favorite menu choice of guests at Viansa's weddings and private dinners, as well as in the deli. You will need to buy the 9x20-inch fresh pasta sheet at a pasta shop.

There are many excellent pasta and marinara sauces available for purchase. However, if you choose to make your own, you can prepare my Marinara Sauce, found with the Cannelloni recipe on page 34. You will only need about half of the amount of the marinara sauce for the Pasta Roll. Save the remaining sauce for another use, or reduce the sauce ingredients by half.

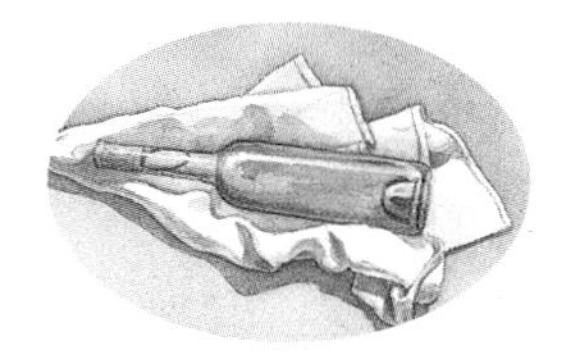

VIANSA WINE SUGGESTION

Sauvignon Blanc, Chardonnay or Cabernet Sauvignon

RISOTTO DI FUNGHI

Mushroom Risotto

How much and how often to stir risotto is an argument that certainly reminds one of how much Italians love to argue about food! I have found that constant stirring is not necessary. I prefer the "deluge and evaporate" method with occasional stirring, as described. Just make sure to use a non-stick skillet so the rice doesn't stick to the bottom.

Homemade chicken broth is easier to make than you think. See page 106 for my easy method.

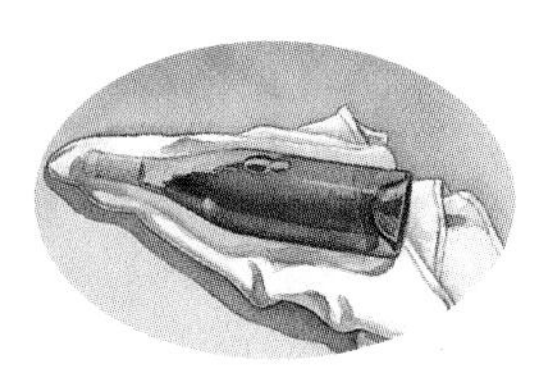

VIANSA WINE SUGGESTION
Reserve Chardonnay or 'Piccolo Toscano' Sangiovese

⅓ ounce dried porcini mushrooms

1 cup hot water

4 tablespoons butter

8 ounces cremini or shiitake mushrooms, cleaned and sliced

4 cups chicken broth, preferably homemade

½ cup dry white wine

1 tablespoon olive oil

¼ cup minced onion

1 tablespoon minced garlic

1½ cups Carnaroli or Arborio rice

⅓ cup freshly grated Parmesan cheese

1 tablespoon chopped Italian parsley

Soak porcini in 1 cup hot water for 15 to 20 minutes, until soft but not soggy. Finely chop porcini and set aside. Strain liquid through two layers of cheesecloth (or a strainer lined with a paper towel) and set aside.

Heat 2 tablespoons of the butter in a large skillet and sauté the fresh mushrooms over medium heat for 3 to 5 minutes, adding chopped porcini during the last minute or so. Remove mushrooms from skillet, set aside and keep warm. Reserve the skillet for further use.

Combine strained porcini liquid, chicken broth and wine in a large sauce pan and bring to a simmer.

Heat the remaining 2 tablespoons butter and the olive oil in the reserved skillet and sauté onion and garlic for 2 minutes. Add rice, stir to coat and sauté 2 to 3 minutes. Add simmering broth, about 1 cup at a time, and continue cooking over medium-high heat until liquid is absorbed and rice is tender but firm, stirring occasionally. Add mushrooms, Parmesan and parsley and stir to combine. Serve hot with an additional sprinkling of Parmesan if desired.

Serves 6 as a first course, 4 as an entrée.

NOTE: I usually make enough risotto so that I'm sure to have leftovers. My family loves the resulting risotto cakes the next day. To make them, combine 1 cup leftover risotto, 2 tablespoons grated Parmesan cheese, 1 beaten egg, 2 teaspoons dried bread crumbs and 2 teaspoons chopped fresh herbs. Form into 2 large patties, wrap in plastic wrap and refrigerate until ready to cook. To cook, sauté patties in 1 tablespoon olive oil until hot throughout.

RISOTTO CON FONTINA E ASPARAGI

Risotto with Fontina and Asparagus

1 bunch asparagus (approximately 1 pound)

2½ cups chicken broth (preferably homemade)

1 cup Arborio or Carnaroli rice

2 teaspoons flour

1 teaspoon salt

⅛ teaspoon white pepper

3 egg yolks, slightly beaten

¾ cup milk

4 ounces Italian fontina cheese, grated

Rinse asparagus. Snap off the woody portion at the bottom of each stalk and cut the spears into half-inch pieces. Immerse into boiling water and simmer briefly until tender yet still firm. Set aside and keep warm.

Pour chicken broth into a large saucepan. Stir rice into broth, bring to boil and simmer 7 to 8 minutes, stirring occasionally. Rice kernels will still be crunchy and there should be excess liquid not yet absorbed by the rice. Stir, cover and remove from heat. Let the rice sit, allowing it to absorb the remainder of the liquid until ready for use, about 5 to 10 minutes. (Cooking time will vary with different brands of rice. Adjust as necessary to obtain the desired results—a very moist, but not "water-logged" rice.)

In a small bowl, blend the flour, salt and pepper with the egg yolks. Stir in the milk and cook in the top of a double boiler. (If you choose not to use a double boiler, use a non-stick saucepan or skillet. Cook over very low heat, whisking constantly, watching very carefully so the eggs don't set. If they do start to set, remove the pan from heat and whisk furiously.) Stir mixture until thickened and smooth. Stir in the cheese and continue to simmer until cheese is melted. Combine asparagus bits, cooked rice and cheese sauce and toss gently to combine. Transfer risotto to a heated serving platter or plates and serve hot.

Serves 8.

Although not made in the traditional manner where rice kernels are browned first, this rich and creamy risotto is typical of the first course served in many Italian homes and restaurants, incorporating tasty morsels of seasonal produce such as asparagus. Use the best Italian fontina cheese you can find, as some American-made fontinas are very bland; otherwise substitute Gruyère.

The extra starch in Arborio and Carnaroli rice makes them especially well-suited to risotto, where a creamy texture is desired.

Homemade chicken broth is easier to make than you think. *See page 106 for my easy method.*

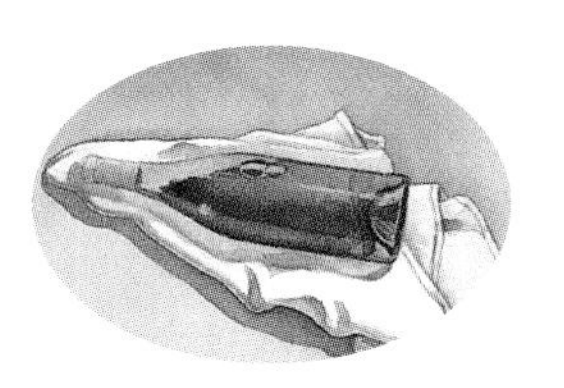

VIANSA WINE SUGGESTION

Reserve Chardonnay or 'Vittoria' Pinot Grigio

Pappardelle with Asparagus and Lemon

PAPPARDELLE CON ASPARAGI E LIMONE

Pappardelle with Asparagus and Lemon

1 bunch pencil-thin asparagus

½ pound pappardelle pasta (or fettucine)

¼ cup freshly squeezed lemon juice (about 2 lemons)

2 tablespoons dry white wine

½ teaspoon salt

1 cup heavy cream

2 tablespoons minced lemon zest

2 tablespoons minced Italian parsley

Snap off the tough ends of the asparagus and cut each stalk into 3 to 4 pieces, slicing on the diagonal. Cook the asparagus in a pot of lightly salted, boiling water for 2 minutes, or until tender but still firm. Immediately place in a bowl of ice water, or under cold running water. After asparagus cools, drain, cover with plastic wrap and set aside.

Cook pasta in a large pot of boiling salted water until al dente (barely tender), about 10 to 12 minutes.

While the pasta is cooking, combine lemon juice and white wine in a small non-stick skillet and cook over medium-high heat until reduced to 2 to 3 tablespoons. Add salt and cream and reduce to about ⅔ cup. Remove from heat and stir in one tablespoon of the lemon zest. Cover to keep warm until the pasta is cooked. When pasta is cooked, drain and return it to the cooking pot. Add asparagus pieces, lemon cream sauce and minced parsley. Toss gently to combine. Transfer to a warm serving platter or plates. Garnish with remaining tablespoon of lemon zest and serve.

Serves 6 to 8.

Lemon zest (lemon peel that excludes the white, pithy part) adds a tasty, piquant zing to many foods. If you don't have the special zester tool that yields skinny little strips, you can use a regular vegetable peeler. Cut the strips you have peeled into ½-inch to 1-inch lengths and then cut the lengths into skinny little sticks about 1/16-inch wide. You can use an even easier method and grate the lemon peel with a grater, although with this method you won't have as pretty a look in the finished dish.

If you are unable to find pappardelle, which are ½-inch to 1-inch wide noodles, use fettucine.

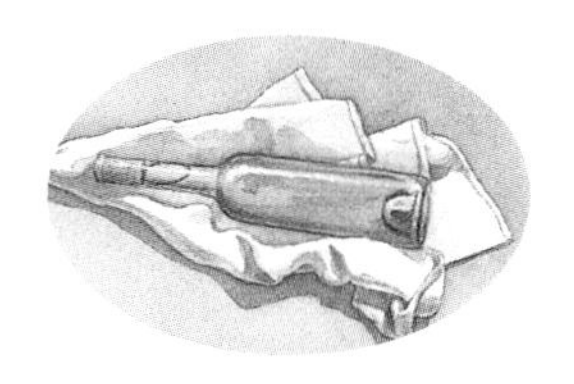

VIANSA WINE SUGGESTION

Sauvignon Blanc or 'Vittoria' Pinot Grigio

RISOTTO AL NEBBIOLO CON PARMIGIANO

Nebbiolo Rice with Parmesan

You can adjust the amounts of wine and water in this recipe, as long as the total amount of liquid remains the same. The more wine you use, the stronger the flavor and the darker the color will be. The quality of Parmesan you use will determine the predominance of cheese flavor. Buy the best you can find. I usually serve this richly flavored rice with lamb or game, such as venison or boar.

2½ cups water

1 cup Viansa Nebbiolo

1 cup Arborio rice

½ teaspoon salt

¼ teaspoon pepper

1 cup freshly grated Parmesan cheese

In a large saucepan, bring water and wine to a boil. Add rice, salt and pepper and stir to prevent sticking. Cover and lower heat, stirring occasionally and removing the lid carefully to release any evaporated alcohol that has collected. (If you use a lot of wine and are near a flame when you open the lid, the accumulated alcohol could ignite, so be careful.)

Cook approximately 15 to 20 minutes, until the rice is tender, but not mushy, and all the liquid is absorbed. Cooking times may vary with different brands of rice. Adjust as necessary to obtain the desired results—you want a very moist but not "water-logged" rice. Add cheese, stir to combine and serve hot.

Makes 6 servings.

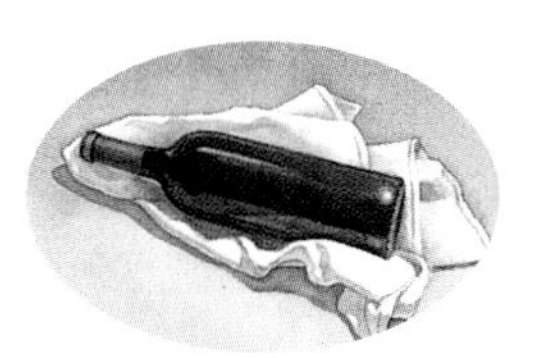

VIANSA WINE SUGGESTION
Nebbiolo

POLENTA SAPORITA

Savory Polenta

4 cups chicken broth (preferably homemade)

1 cup polenta

½ pound fresh brown mushrooms

4 tablespoons Viansa Extra Virgin Olive Oil

4 large cloves garlic, minced

1 can (4 ounces) diced green chiles, drained

½ cup diced roasted red bell peppers

8 ounces Asiago cheese, cut into ⅛-inch cubes

½ cup freshly grated Asiago cheese (1½ ounces)

Bring chicken broth to a boil in a large saucepan. Slowly drizzle in polenta, stirring continuously. When broth returns to a boil, lower heat and cook polenta, stirring frequently, about 15 to 20 minutes, until polenta loses its grittiness.

Meanwhile, brush or rinse mushrooms and thinly slice. Heat 3 tablespoons olive oil in a large sauté pan and sauté mushrooms and garlic over medium-high heat until mushrooms have released their liquid and it has evaporated. When polenta is soft and creamy, stir in the mushrooms and garlic, the drained green chiles, diced peppers and cubed Asiago.

Pour into a decorative, shallow serving dish, top with grated Asiago and place under the broiler until cheese has melted and top is light brown. Serve with grilled meat, chicken or fish.

Serves 12.

To serve with sautéed chicken or pork chops, omit the chiles when making the polenta, pour onto a serving platter and top with cooked meat. You may also want to spoon some marinara or pasta sauce on top. Either my Marinara Sauce recipe on page 34 or my Soffrito Sauce recipe on page 33 would be an excellent addition.

For grilled polenta, pour cooked polenta in a single layer into a 9x13-inch baking dish. Chill a couple of hours until polenta is firm, then cut into squares, rectangles or triangles. Grill (or sauté in olive oil) until lightly browned and hot throughout.

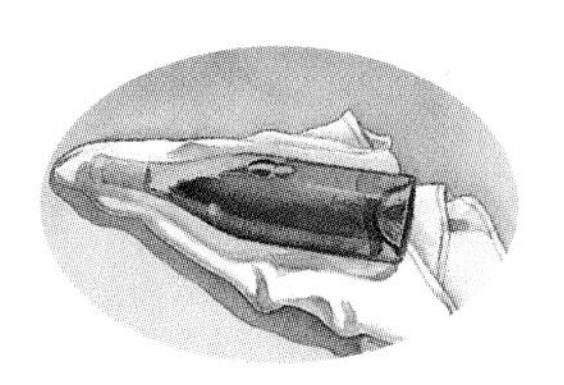

VIANSA WINE SUGGESTION

'Riserva Anatra Bianco' Trebbiano or Cabernet Sauvignon

Polenta Lasagna

LASAGNA DI POLENTA

Polenta Lasagna

4 cups water

1 cup polenta

2 tablespoons minced fresh thyme

2 tablespoons minced fresh basil

2 tablespoons minced Italian parsley

1 tablespoon olive oil

¾ pound mozzarella, sliced into 16 slices

½ cup kalamata olives, pitted and halved

½ cup roasted garlic cloves (see sidebar)

1 cup basil pesto (see sidebar)

4 medium Roma tomatoes, sliced (about ½ pound)

3 cups marinara or red pasta sauce (see sidebar)

Bring water to a boil in a large saucepan. Slowly drizzle in polenta and herbs, stirring continuously. When water returns to a boil, lower heat and cook polenta, stirring frequently, about 15 to 20 minutes, until polenta loses its grittiness.

Preheat oven to 375°F.

Using 1 tablespoon olive oil, grease a 9x13-inch baking dish. Spread ⅓ of the hot polenta on the bottom of the baking dish. Layer half of the mozzarella slices on the polenta and evenly distribute the kalamata olives and roasted garlic over the mozzarella. Spread half of the remaining polenta over the top and spread the basil pesto over it. Spread the remaining polenta over the pesto and top with remaining mozzarella and the sliced tomatoes.

Bake for 30 minutes to heat throughout. Remove from the oven and cut into 3-inch squares. For an elegant presentation, serve each square on a plate covered with ¼ cup heated pasta sauce (or, if you prefer, serve the pasta sauce drizzled over the top of the lasagna).

Makes 12 squares.

A very popular dish in our Marketplace, the Polenta Lasagna uses both our own basil pesto and red pasta sauce. You may substitute purchased pesto and sauce, or follow the recipe for pesto on page 16 (Bruschetta with Oysters and Pesto) and half of the Marinara Sauce recipe on page 34 (Cannelloni). For my quick method of roasting garlic, turn to page 19 (Brie with Roasted Garlic).

VIANSA WINE SUGGESTION
'Piccolo Toscano' Sangiovese or Chardonnay

Piatti del Giorno

Main Dishes

Here in Sonoma we have access to the freshest seafood

and the finest meats in the world.

Whether we are grilling lamb with fresh rosemary beneath a starlit summer sky

or savoring a steaming bowl of Tuscan seafood stew in front of a roaring fire,

we are grateful for the bounty of our valley.

Villagers tend vines on the hillsides of Farneta under the watchful eye of a Sebastiani ancestor.

CHILI PICCANTE ALL' ITALIANA

Spicy Italian Chili

This is one of the few dishes where I use dried seasonings. I much prefer the flavor, texture, aroma and even the sight of fresh herbs. However, in this case, dried herbs are just fine. Just be sure they are not stale! Stored in a cool, dry place, dried herbs have a shelf life of about six months. If stored near a hot oven or stove, they are flavorless in a week.

If you want to dry your own fresh herbs you can microwave them layered between several thicknesses of paper towels for 2 to 3 minutes — or lay them upside down in a small paper bag for a few weeks until dry.

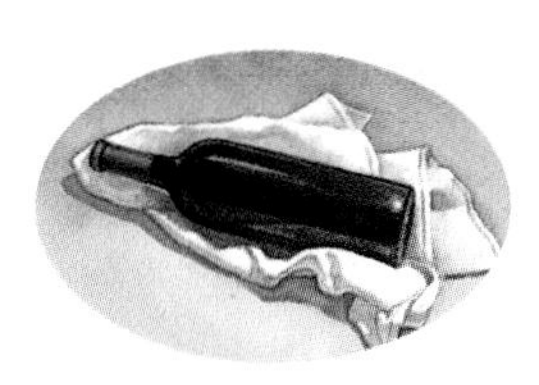

VIANSA WINE SUGGESTION
Prindelo or
'Piccolo Toscano' Sangiovese

⅓ cup olive oil

2 red bell peppers, cored, seeded and chopped

3 large yellow or white onions, sliced into half rings, ⅛-inch thick

12 cloves garlic, minced

10 spicy Italian sausages (about 2 pounds), peeled and broken into large pieces

2 cans (28 ounces each) Italian whole tomatoes, including liquid

1 can (6 ounces) tomato paste

4 cans (15 ounces each) red kidney beans, drained

2 cups hearty red wine

3 tablespoons dried Italian seasoning

2 teaspoons salt

½ teaspoon pepper

2 dashes Tabasco sauce (or more if desired)

1½ cups freshly grated Parmesan cheese

Heat the olive oil in a large soup pot over medium heat. Sauté the peppers, onions and garlic until limp, about 10 minutes. Remove from the pot and set aside. Sauté the sausage over medium-high heat until light brown, about 15 minutes. Discard any excess grease. Return the vegetables to the pot. Add the tomatoes, tomato paste, kidney beans, wine, Italian seasoning, salt, pepper and Tabasco. Simmer over low heat until thickened, about 2 hours, stirring occasionally. Serve hot, sprinkled with the Parmesan cheese.

Serves 6.

ARISTA ALL'ARENTINA

Garlic and Herb-Wrapped Pork Roast

1 dozen sprigs fresh tarragon, thyme or rosemary (or a combination)

5 to 6 pound pork blade or shoulder roast

¼ cup olive oil (approximately)

2 teaspoons salt

1 teaspoon pepper

12 cloves garlic, thinly sliced

Cheesecloth

2 cups dry white wine

Preheat oven to 350°F.

Rinse herbs and remove any old, woody stems and leaves. Trim excess fat from the roast. Rub the roast generously with olive oil. Sprinkle with salt and pepper. Spread out enough cheesecloth to wrap one layer around the roast.

Place garlic slices and herb sprigs all over the roast and tightly wrap the roast with cheesecloth to hold it all in. The cheesecloth will adhere to the oiled meat just fine, requiring no tying. Insert a meat thermometer into the center of the thickest part of the roast. Place the roast on a rack in a shallow roasting pan (such as a broiler pan with a cake rack) and pour the wine into the pan.

Roast pork until thermometer registers 170°F. This takes approximately two hours, but be guided by the temperature, not the time. Roast should be tender and juicy, not tough and dry. Let the roast sit for about 15 minutes before unwrapping and carving.

To serve, remove the cheesecloth and discard. Discard herb sprigs but save the garlic—it's sweet and tasty! Slice the roast and top slices with the natural juice that has accumulated. Accompany with Viansa Peperoni Rossi Saporiti, our savory Red Pepper Relish.

Serves 8 to 10.

The typical Tuscan-style pork roast with garlic and rosemary, called Arista All'Arentina, is usually a spit-roasted pork loin. I prefer a pork blade or shoulder roast, cooked slowly in a conventional oven so that it stays juicy and succulent.

I developed this unusual method of roasting meat wrapped in cheesecloth to retain the meat's juices. Follow this temperature guideline and you'll have a tender, juicy, flavorful roast.

VIANSA WINE SUGGESTION

Prindelo or 'Riserva Anatra Bianco' Trebbiano

Pork Tenderloins with Orange Sauce

FILETTI DI MAIALE CON SALSA ALL'ARANCIA

Pork Tenderloins with Orange Sauce

PORK

2 pork tenderloins, approximately 1 pound each, excess fat removed

2 teaspoons freshly ground black pepper

2 tablespoons olive oil

ORANGE SAUCE

10 strips orange zest, approximately 2 inches long and ½-inch wide (about 2 medium oranges)

4 tablespoons butter

½ cup finely minced carrot

¾ cup finely minced onion

½ cup finely minced celery

½ cup Viansa Blood Orange Vinegar (or white wine vinegar)

1 cup freshly squeezed orange juice

2 teaspoons sugar

1½ cups white wine

½ cup orange liqueur

1 tablespoon + 1 teaspoon minced fresh dill

2 teaspoons flour

PORK TENDERLOINS

Lightly sprinkle 1 teaspoon black pepper over each tenderloin on all sides. Heat 2 tablespoons olive oil in a large non-stick sauté pan over medium heat. Increase the heat to medium-high and sauté the pork 6 minutes, turning to brown evenly. Lower heat to medium-low and sauté another 4 minutes on each side (total cooking time 14 minutes). The resulting meat is medium-rare. If you prefer it medium to well done, increase the cooking time slightly. Make a small cut with a sharp knife to check for desired doneness. Slightly undercook as it will continue to cook while you prepare the sauce. Remove pork and wrap in aluminum foil to keep warm.

ORANGE SAUCE

In a small saucepan of boiling water, gently boil the orange zest for 15 minutes to soften. Cool slightly and cut the orange zest into thin matchsticks. In a large non-stick pan, sauté the carrots, onion and celery in butter for 5 minutes. Add the orange strips, vinegar, orange juice, sugar, wine and liqueur. Boil over low heat for 15 to 20 minutes until it reduces and thickens. Add 1 teaspoon of the dill, sprinkle in the flour and stir to combine and thicken slightly.

To serve, pour half the orange sauce onto a large heated platter and spread over the surface. Slice each warm tenderloin in 12 slices and place on top of the orange sauce. Pour remaining sauce over the meat and sprinkle with remaining tablespoon of fresh dill. Serve immediately.

Serves 6 to 8 (3 to 4 small slices per person).

When making this dish, our friend Patrizia, who lives in a centuries-old home in Terontola, Tuscany, uses the traditional soffrito, a sautéed mixture of minced onions, carrots and celery which is a base used in many Tuscan dishes.

If you do not care for pork, a small turkey breast makes a fine substitute.

VIANSA WINE SUGGESTION
Nebbiolo,
Reserve Chardonnay or
'Imbianco' Barbera Rosé

SCALLOPINI ELISABETTA

Elizabeth's Veal Scallopini

When Sam and I were expecting our daughter Elizabeth, we found ourselves in an old-fashioned, dimly lit Italian restaurant on Central Park in New York. We had just received a call from the doctor, announcing that our baby was to be a girl! As we settled into the deep booth and perused the menu, we were glowing. Suddenly a big smile crossed Sam's face and he set the menu down. He had found an excellent entree choice — Scallopini Elisabetta— Veal Elizabeth. "We already have one queen in the family," he said, referring to my birth name, Victoria. "I think we should have another." And Elizabeth it was to be!

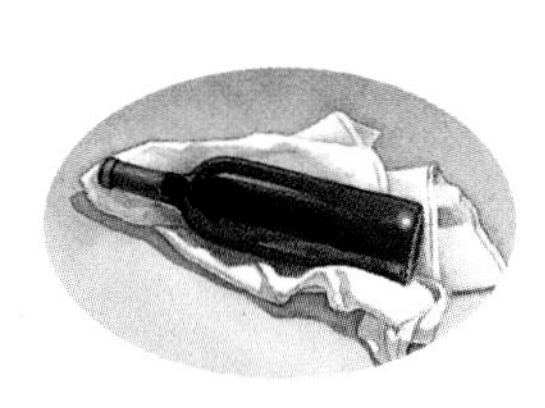

VIANSA WINE SUGGESTION

Reserve Cabernet Sauvignon or 'Cento per Cento' Chardonnay

12 thin (about ⅛-inch thick) slices veal scallopini (about 1 pound)

2 tablespoons butter

2 tablespoons olive oil

Flour for dredging

2 large cloves garlic, minced

4 anchovy filets, minced

2 dozen kalamata olives, pitted and halved

4 Italian plum tomatoes, (canned), chopped

½ cup white wine

½ teaspoon salt

½ teaspoon freshly ground black pepper

6 leaves fresh basil, chopped

1 tablespoon minced Italian parsley

2 tablespoons capers

If scallopini slices are surrounded by a thin membrane, snip through it with a sharp knife to prevent the veal from curling when cooking. Heat butter and oil in a large sauté pan. Dredge the scallopini slices in flour and shake off excess. Over medium heat, sauté scallopini for 1 minute on each side. Remove and set aside.

In the same pan, over medium-low heat, sauté garlic, anchovies and olives for 1 to 2 minutes. Add tomatoes and mash with a fork. Stir in the wine, salt and pepper, reduce heat and cook over low heat for 5 minutes. Add the basil, parsley and capers and simmer a few minutes more. Add scallopini and cook only until hot. Serve immediately.

Serves 4.

VITELLO TONNATO

Rosemary Roast Veal with Tonnato Sauce

6 to 8 pound leg of veal, boned and butterflied (I have the butcher do it)

2 to 3 tablespoons olive oil

½ cup chopped fresh rosemary

12 cloves garlic, peeled and sliced

½ teaspoon salt

¼ teaspoon freshly ground black pepper

6 slices bacon

1 to 2 cups red wine

TONNATO SAUCE

1 can (about 6 ounces) water-packed tuna or albacore, drained

6 anchovy filets

2 tablespoons capers

2 tablespoons white wine

2 tablespoons freshly squeezed lemon juice

½ teaspoon salt

⅛ teaspoon white pepper

2 cups mayonnaise (homemade is best)

3 to 4 hard-cooked eggs, sliced

Preheat oven to 325°F.

Remove any excess fat from veal. Rub all sides of the meat generously with olive oil. Lay the meat flat with the membrane side down. Cover the top surface with most of the rosemary leaves and garlic slices. Roll the roast tightly and tie together with kitchen string. Place the rest of the garlic and rosemary on the top of the roast. Sprinkle with salt and pepper and cover the top with bacon slices.

Place meat in a shallow roasting pan, pour 1 cup of the wine in the bottom and roast until meat thermometer reaches 150°F, approximately 3 hours. Add more wine if necessary, so that the bottom of the pan remains covered. After 2 hours remove the bacon from the top.

Remove the roast from the oven, transfer it to a serving platter or cutting board and let it sit for 15 to 20 minutes before slicing (I cover it loosely with foil to keep it warm). Place roasting pan on the stove over medium-high heat. Add ½ cup wine and scrape the bottom of the pan to loosen any bits of meat. To serve, slice the roast into ½-inch thick slices. Pour pan juices over the slices or pass at the table. Or, chill veal and serve with Tonnato Sauce.

Serves 8 to 10.

TONNATO SAUCE

In a food processor or blender, purée tuna, anchovies, capers, wine, lemon juice, salt and pepper. Add mayonnaise and blend just long enough to thoroughly combine all the ingredients.

Serve with thinly sliced cold veal and garnish with hard-cooked egg slices.

Most people think of veal as an expensive, special occasion meat. Actually, leg of veal is very reasonably priced. It is quite lean with little waste, and it is also richly flavored, so individual portions don't need to be large.

This veal roast is equally delicious served cold and I have included a recipe for the classic Italian Tonnato Sauce to enjoy with it. The sauce recipe is enough to be served with the entire roast. If you are using it only with leftovers, you might want to reduce the amount you prepare.

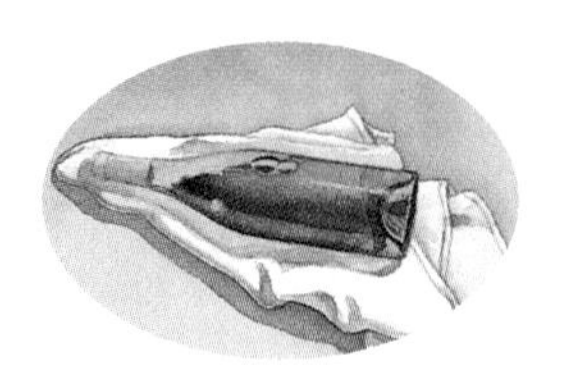

VIANSA WINE SUGGESTION

'Riserva Anatra Bianco' Trebbiano, 'Thalia' Sangiovese or 'Augusto' Barbera

Grilled Rosemary Lamb Steaks

FETTE DI AGNELLO CON ROSMARINO

Grilled Rosemary Lamb Steaks

1 leg of lamb (about 6 pounds), boned, or 12 boneless lamb sirloin steaks (about 5 to 6 ounces each)

1 can (12 ounces) frozen cherry or raspberry (or combination) juice concentrate

½ cup water

1 cup full-bodied red wine

¼ cup minced fresh rosemary

4 cloves garlic, minced

3 or 4 sprigs rosemary, for grilling (optional)

Cut the boned leg of lamb into approximately 12 pieces about ¾-inch thick, roughly 5 ounces each, that have little or no skin, sinew, tendons or membranes. If you have a piece that is an odd shape, butterfly it (make a slice partially through the middle, lay it open and pound with a kitchen mallet to flatten out to ¾-inch thickness). Try to cut all steaks to a similar thickness. Save any remaining meat for another use (perhaps skewered with onions and mushrooms and grilled along with the steak).

In a large, shallow glass baking dish, combine juice, water, wine, rosemary and garlic. Place steaks in the marinade, turning to coat both sides. Cover with plastic wrap and refrigerate at least 1 to 2 hours (overnight is even better), turning the meat once.

TO GRILL ON BARBECUE: Place meat over medium-low coals for 6 minutes on first side. Turn and grill second side 3 minutes. The thinner steaks will be cooked medium-well and the thicker steaks will be medium-rare. If using pre-cut steaks, adjust cooking time as necessary for the thickness of the meat. Add sprigs of fresh rosemary to the coals just before removing the meat. The rosemary smoke will add a wonderful, subtle flavor to the meat.

TO GRILL IN SKILLET: Drain the lamb steaks and pat with paper towels to remove excess marinade. Preheat a large skillet over medium heat. When the skillet is sizzling hot, add 1 to 2 tablespoons of olive oil. Heat it briefly and add steaks. Sauté 5 minutes, reduce heat to medium-low, turn meat and sauté an additional 3 minutes. If using pre-cut steaks, adjust cooking time as necessary for the thickness of the meat. Remove steaks to a platter and keep warm. Add ½ cup red wine to the skillet and cook over high heat for 2 to 3 minutes to reduce the pan juices. Scrape to loosen and incorporate any meat bits. Pour over lamb steaks and serve.

Serves 8.

I use a boneless leg of lamb instead of pre-cut chops or steaks, as I am able to create beautiful little steaks with no fat, bones, chewy membranes or tendons. It does take a little more time, but with a sharp knife and an adventurous spirit, I find the results are worth it. I prefer these lamb steaks barbecued, but skillet grilling also works very well.

If you are fortunate enough to have access to game, try preparing it with this marinade, and you will be thrilled by the "oohs" and "aahs" from your lucky guests. Venison, boar, bear or even goat will lose its gamey flavor and become flavorful, succulent and tender.

VIANSA WINE SUGGESTION

'Augusto' Barbera or 'Ossidiana' Cabernet Franc/ Cabernet Sauvignon

AGNELLO ALLA FIORENTINA ALLA GRIGLIA

Grilled Florentine Lamb, Sonoma Style

Herbs have always played a major role in Italian cuisine, and it would be hard to imagine Italian food without them. You will notice throughout this book that almost all recipes call for fresh herbs. Dried herbs have lost their essential oils, and thus much of their flavor. I use them only when fresh herbs won't achieve the results I'm looking for, such as flavoring a long-simmered stew or soup.

VIANSA WINE SUGGESTION
Prindelo or Cabernet Sauvignon

¾ cup olive oil

½ cup Viansa Cabernet Sauvignon Vinegar

½ cup dry red wine

1 can (4 ounces) diced green chiles

6 cloves garlic, minced

1 teaspoon minced Italian parsley

1 teaspoon minced fresh basil

1 teaspoon minced fresh marjoram leaves

1 teaspoon minced fresh rosemary

2 tablespoons Viansa Hot Sweet Mustard or Rosemary Mustard

1 leg of lamb (6 to 8 pounds), boned and butterflied (I have the butcher do it)

1 can (8 ounces) tomato sauce

3 tablespoons honey

Combine the oil, vinegar, wine, chiles, garlic, parsley, basil, marjoram, rosemary and mustard and mix well. Trim excess fat and membranes from the lamb and place it in a shallow glass baking dish. Pour the marinade mixture over it and turn to coat thoroughly. Cover with plastic wrap and refrigerate overnight, turning once.

To barbecue, remove the meat from the marinade. Prepare a basting sauce by blending the tomato sauce and honey into the marinade and mixing well. Barbecue the marinated lamb over a double layer of hot coals for 8 to 10 minutes on each side, basting frequently. Since butterflied leg of lamb is irregular in shape, the outer, thinner pieces will cook in less time. The center will be medium-rare and the outer pieces will be medium to well done, depending on their thickness. Adjust cooking time to your preference.

Serves 8 to 10.

BISTECCA ALLA FIORENTINA ALLA SAM

Sam's Marinated Steak

MARINADE

1 cup fresh thyme leaves (stripped from twigs)

1½ cups fresh rosemary (stripped from twigs)

½ cup olive oil

¼ cup Viansa Cabernet Sauvignon Vinegar

½ cup dry red wine

2 tablespoons Viansa Hot Sweet Mustard

3 cloves garlic

8 to 10 rib, market or New York steaks

Purée all the marinade ingredients in a food processor or blender until creamy (marinade is best if made 24 hours ahead of use to marry flavors).

Trim any excess fat from the steaks and cover both sides with marinade. Place steaks in a shallow glass baking dish. Cover with plastic wrap and refrigerate for 2 to 4 hours before barbecuing.

Serves 8 to 10.

Bistecca alla Fiorentina is THE steak of Italy. Traditionally, it is a more simply prepared T-bone or Porterhouse — salted, peppered and drizzled with olive oil. But Florentines use so many herbs that I took the liberty of expanding the definition a bit. Especially since these steaks are sporting THE marinade of our family.

The basis of this marinade is one Sam created many years ago to impress his dates with his barbecuing skills. It worked on me! It is also terrific with chicken or prawns.

VIANSA WINE SUGGESTION

'Riserva Anatra Rosso' Cabernet Sauvignon,
Cabernet Sauvignon or
'Augusto' Barbera

Rolled Beef with Artichoke Stuffing

FALSO MAGRO

Rolled Beef with Artichoke Stuffing

Falso Magro means "false lean" in Italian. This dish is so named because it appears lean, but is actually a substantial entree made from beef or veal rolled around a rich filling.

½ pound ground veal

½ pound ground pork

½ pound prosciutto, diced

½ cup diced fontina cheese (2 ounces)

½ cup diced Asiago cheese (2 ounces)

6 cloves garlic, minced

½ cup chopped fennel

2 cups marinated artichokes, cut into 1-inch pieces (reserve oil in jar)

½ cup coarsely chopped Italian parsley

½ cup minced fresh sage leaves

1 egg, beaten

1 tablespoon dried Italian seasoning

¼ teaspoon salt

¼ teaspoon pepper

1½ to 2 pounds flank steak

2 hard-cooked eggs

½ cup dry red wine

In a large bowl combine veal, pork, prosciutto, cheeses, garlic, fennel, artichokes, herbs, egg, Italian seasoning, salt and pepper and mix well.

Trim excess fat from flank steak and pound to approximately ⅛-inch thickness. (This takes a few minutes, but is important to the recipe. Use a kitchen mallet or a heavy flat weight such as a wine bottle.) Spread stuffing over meat, covering it completely. Lay egg quarters down center, lengthwise, and roll meat around stuffing without overlapping. Tie with kitchen string at one inch intervals to hold securely; if any stuffing escapes, carefully push it back in.

Heat a large heavy skillet over medium-high heat. Add ¼ cup of the reserved artichoke oil. Heat oil and add stuffed beef roll to hot oil and brown on all sides. Add wine, cover and cook over low heat for 45 minutes. Turn beef roll over halfway through cooking. When cooked, transfer meat to a serving platter and remove the string. Slice and serve with the pan juices. The Falso Magro roll is also terrific served on buffets, at picnics or even cold the next day.

NOTE: If you have any stuffing left over, pat it into sausage shapes and wrap tightly in foil. Bake at 325°F for 35 minutes. Serve alongside Falso Magro.

Serves 8 to 10.

VIANSA WINE SUGGESTION

'Ossidiana' Cabernet Franc/ Cabernet Sauvignon or Prindelo

POLLO FARE MERENDA

Picnic Chicken Smokies

These chicken rolls are a favorite for picnics, since they taste great served at room temperature. They are also great for a casual buffet where it is difficult to keep food piping hot.

6 large chicken thighs

6 teaspoons Viansa Hot Sweet Mustard

¼ cup minced white onion

6 teaspoons freshly grated Parmesan cheese

1 teaspoon salt

½ teaspoon pepper

12 small (1-inch) or 6 large (3-inch) smoked sausages (available in deli meat section of supermarkets; they resemble miniature hot dogs)

¼ cup dry white wine

3 slices bacon, cut in half

❧Remove the bone from each thigh by running a small sharp knife along the bone, and then cutting the meat away from it in one piece. Remove any cartilage and lay out each thigh, skin side down. Spread one teaspoon mustard on each thigh and sprinkle each with 2 teaspoons onion, one teaspoon Parmesan cheese, and a dash of salt and pepper.

❧Preheat oven to 350°F.

❧Place 2 small or one large smoky sausage in the center of each thigh. Fold the thigh around the sausage and tie it in 2 or 3 places with kitchen string (or tuck tightly into a perfectly sized oven-proof baking dish). Trim the sausage if necessary. Place the thighs on a rack in an oven-proof baking pan, skin side up, and pour the wine in the bottom of the pan. Top each thigh with half a slice of bacon.

❧Bake for 15 minutes. Remove the bacon and bake 10 minutes more, until browned. If not serving immediately, let the thighs sit for 15 minutes before removing the string.

Serves 6.

VIANSA WINE SUGGESTION
'Di Pacomio' Aleatico, Sauvignon Blanc or 'Imbianco' Barbera Rosé

POLLO AL CACCIATORE

Chicken Cacciatore

3 tablespoons olive oil

1 large frying chicken, excess fat removed, cut into pieces

2 large onions, chopped

½ pound chanterelle, portobello or cremini mushrooms, cleaned and sliced

8 cloves garlic, minced

1 can (28 ounces) Italian plum tomatoes, undrained

1 tablespoon Viansa Olive Anchovy Pesto (optional)

2 marinated Italian peperoncini, minced

1 can (8 ounces) tomato sauce

1 teaspoon salt

¼ teaspoon pepper

2 tablespoons minced fresh oregano

¼ cup minced fresh basil

¼ cup minced Italian parsley

2 bay leaves

¾ cup dry red wine

½ cup freshly grated Parmesan cheese

Heat oil in a large, deep skillet and sauté chicken over medium-high heat until golden brown, about 10 minutes on each side. Remove chicken from the skillet and set aside. Add onions to the skillet and sauté for 3 to 4 minutes. Add the mushrooms and garlic to the onions, cooking another 5 minutes. Add all remaining ingredients except the wine and cheese. Stir to blend, breaking up the tomatoes with a fork. Return chicken to sauce, cover and simmer for 30 minutes. Stir in the wine and cook, uncovered, for an additional 15 minutes.

Remove the bay leaves and arrange chicken on a hot platter. Pour the sauce over it and sprinkle with grated Parmesan cheese. Chicken Cacciatore makes a full meal when served on a bed of polenta or pasta.

Serves 4 to 6.

There is no traditional dish by this name in Italy. "Chicken Cacciatore" is an American creation that began appearing on menus in Italian restaurants after World War II. Its name means chicken "hunter style". Its origin relates to hunters being far away from sources of supplies and making do with what was on hand, such as forest mushrooms, roots and wild greens — much as both war-torn Italian and transient soldiers were forced to do. Modern, authentic Italian cookbooks do not carry recipes for cacciatore, although some of my older Italian cookbooks by Italian-Americans do have recipes.

VIANSA WINE SUGGESTION

Nebbiolo or 'Piccolo Toscano' Sangiovese

Grilled Prosciutto-Wrapped Chicken and Pepper Skewers

SPIEDINI DI INVOLTINI DI POLLO AL PROSCIUTTO

Grilled Prosciutto-Wrapped Chicken and Pepper Skewers

MARINADE

2 tablespoons minced garlic

1 tablespoon minced fresh sage leaves

1 tablespoon minced fresh rosemary

⅓ cup Viansa Balsamic Vinegar

1 cup olive oil

Salt and pepper to taste

CHICKEN SKEWERS

4 boneless, skinless chicken breasts (6 ounces each), cut into four equal pieces

1 red bell pepper, cored, seeded and cut into 2-inch squares

1 yellow bell pepper, cored, seeded and cut into 2-inch squares

1 small bulb fennel, trimmed and cut into eight wedges

16 thin slices prosciutto

4 wooden skewers (10 to 12-inches long)

In a small bowl, whisk together the marinade ingredients. Divide the marinade in half. In a medium-sized glass bowl, toss the chicken pieces with half of the marinade. In another medium-sized glass bowl, toss the peppers and fennel with the other half of the marinade. Cover both bowls tightly with plastic wrap and refrigerate a minimum of 3 hours, tossing occasionally. (The longer the chicken and vegetables marinate, the more flavor they acquire —8 to 12 hours is even better.) Rub the skewers against each other on all surfaces to remove any splinters and immerse in cold water to soak for as long as the chicken marinates.

To grill, remove chicken from marinade and wrap a slice of prosciutto around each piece. Thread each piece onto the skewers, alternating the chicken with pieces of peppers and fennel, until all the ingredients are used. Reserve the vegetable marinade for basting. Season skewers with salt and pepper and grill over moderate heat for 3 to 4 minutes per side, rotating frequently and basting with the reserved marinade.

Serves 4.

These little Involtini—or "bundles of flavor"—are traditionally prepared in the reverse order. The flattened chicken breast is wrapped around the prosciutto stuffing. We prefer these tasty little bundles with the flavor of crisp prosciutto on the outside, so it's the first thing you bite into.

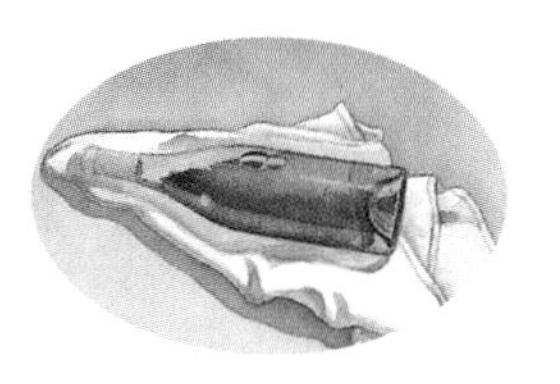

VIANSA WINE SUGGESTION

'Riserva Anatra Bianco' Trebbiano or 'Riserva Anatra Rosso' Cabernet Sauvignon

Chicken Saltimbocca with Pesto Sauce

POLLO SALTIMBOCCA CON PESTO

Chicken Saltimbocca with Pesto Sauce

PESTO
8 cloves garlic

1 cup Italian parsley

1 cup fresh basil leaves

⅓ cup olive oil

2 tablespoons chopped walnuts

2 tablespoons freshly grated Parmesan cheese

¼ teaspoon salt

Dash of pepper

CHICKEN
8 large chicken thighs, boned

8 very thin slices fontina cheese, cut to the size of boned and opened chicken thighs

8 very thin slices prosciutto, cut to the size of boned and opened thigh

Salt and pepper to taste

SAUCE
1 cup whipping cream

PESTO

Combine garlic, parsley, basil, olive oil, walnuts, grated Parmesan cheese, salt and pepper in a food processor or blender and purée until smooth.

CHICKEN

Preheat oven to 375°F.

Lay out each chicken thigh, skin side down. Spread each thigh with 2 tablespoons pesto (reserve remaining pesto for the sauce) and top with a slice of cheese and a slice of prosciutto. Roll up each thigh to enclose filling and place tightly together, seam side down, in a small, shallow baking dish, about 8x8-inches square. Sprinkle with salt and pepper and bake uncovered for 25 to 30 minutes.

SAUCE

Whip the cream until it is soft and thick, about the consistency of a thin mayonnaise. Fold in the reserved pesto. Cover tightly with plastic wrap and keep the sauce at room temperature until ready for use.

To serve, transfer chicken thighs to a serving platter and top each piece with 2 tablespoons of the room temperature sauce (heating sauce will turn the pesto brown), or pass sauce at the table.

Serves 8.

I love the flavor of basil pesto and use it frequently in recipes for Viansa as well as for my family. Although Saltimbocca usually refers to a complex and delicious veal dish, meaning literally "jump in the mouth," I devised this pesto-flavored California version with chicken for a change of pace.

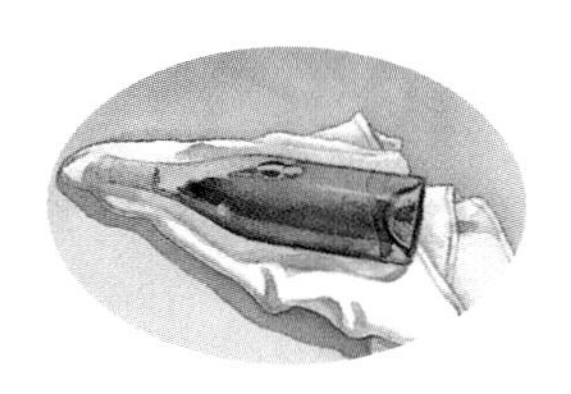

VIANSA WINE SUGGESTION
Reserve Chardonnay or Nebbiolo

POLLO VIANSA ALLA GRIGLIA

Viansa's Grilled Chicken

Our Grilled Chicken Panino —or sandwich—has always been the most popular deli choice at Viansa's deli, Lo Spuntino's deli and the outdoor grill at Viansa. Deceptive in its simplicity, the secret lies in the marinade. After much thought, I decided to include the secret for making your own Panini at home.

MARINADE

2 tablespoons minced garlic (about 8 cloves)

2 tablespoons minced fresh rosemary

½ cup Viansa Balsamic Vinegar

2 tablespoons Viansa Cabernet Sauvignon Wine Vinegar

¾ cup Viansa Extra Virgin Olive Oil

12 skinless and boneless chicken breasts (6 to 8 ounces each)

Combine all marinade ingredients in a food processor or blender and purée until very well blended. Thoroughly coat the chicken breasts with marinade, place them in a covered container and refrigerate overnight. Barbecue over medium coals, about 4 to 6 inches from heat, until golden brown, tender and juicy in the center. Be careful not to overcook.

Serves 8 to 12.

NOTE: To make your own Viansa panino on foccacia bread, use my Foccacia Bread recipe on page 113. Slice chicken breasts into ½-inch thick slices, spread Viansa Basil Pesto Aioli on the bread and add slices of provolone cheese, sun-dried tomatoes and lettuce. You can now enjoy Viansa's specialty! All you need to complete the meal is a glass of our fine Italian-style wine, a little Italian music and a gorgeous hillside view of wetlands.

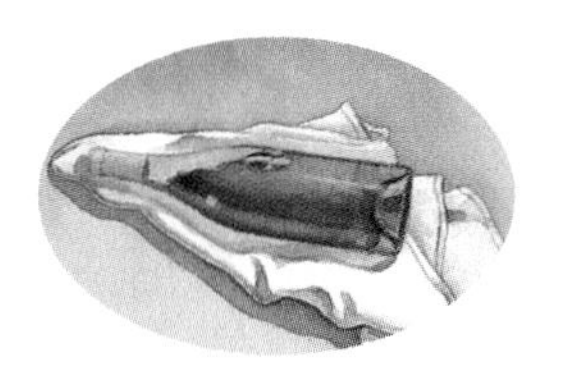

VIANSA WINE SUGGESTION
Chardonnay, Nebbiolo or 'Imbianco' Barbera Rosé

PESCE SPADA, GNOCCHI E FUNGHI

Swordfish, Gnocchi and Chanterelles

5 tablespoons Viansa Extra Virgin Olive Oil

12 small cloves garlic

⅓ pound chanterelle mushrooms, cleaned and sliced

1 package (12 ounces) potato gnocchi

2 pounds swordfish, sturgeon, shark or other firm-fleshed fish, cut into ¾-inch cubes

1 large bunch fresh spinach, rinsed, stems removed, sliced into ½-inch ribbons (about 2 cups)

1 basket cherry tomatoes (about 2 cups)

½ cup fresh basil leaves, sliced into ½-inch strips

Salt and pepper to taste

In a large non-stick sauté pan, heat 3 tablespoons of the olive oil over medium heat and sauté the garlic cloves for 2 minutes, turning to cook evenly. Increase heat, add mushrooms, toss and sauté another 2 minutes. Remove and set aside.

Bring a large saucepan of water to a boil. Add the gnocchi and boil until they rise to the surface, about 2 to 4 minutes. Remove gnocchi with a slotted spoon, drain well and pat dry.

In a large, non-stick sauté pan, heat 1 tablespoon olive oil and sauté gnocchi over medium-high heat. Toss occasionally to lightly brown, about 5 minutes. Remove to a large shallow serving dish and place in 150°F oven to keep warm.

Add another tablespoon olive oil to the sauté pan and sauté swordfish cubes over high heat 3 to 4 minutes, until barely cooked. Add mushroom mixture, spinach, tomatoes, basil leaves and salt and pepper. Stir over high heat until the spinach has wilted, about 3 to 4 minutes. Remove the gnocchi from oven and add swordfish mixture to it. Combine gently with two large spoons and serve hot.

Serves 6.

Exotic mushrooms, such as chanterelles, are now widely available in supermarkets. I encourage you to experiment with them in all your favorite mushroom recipes! Take care when cleaning mushrooms, as they can easily become waterlogged. I prefer to clean them with a soft brush or paper towel, using little or no water.

Uncooked gnocchi are available in sealed packages usually found in the deli section of many markets.

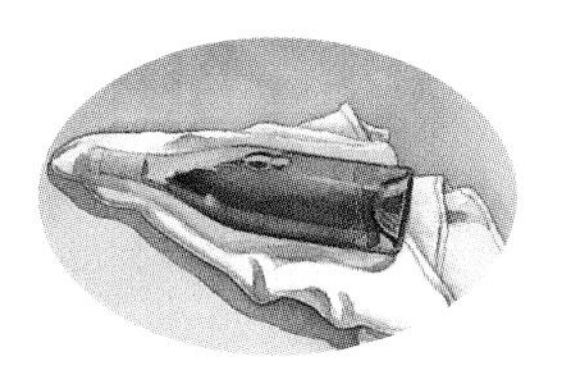

VIANSA WINE SUGGESTION

'Riserva Anatra Bianco' Trebbiano or Sauvignon Blanc

Lemon Roasted Chicken with Lemon-Honey Sauce

POLLO AL LIMONE

Lemon Roasted Chicken with Lemon-Honey Sauce

1 frying chicken (about 3 pounds)

½ cup white wine

2 cups freshly squeezed lemon juice (about 9 lemons)

1 teaspoon salt

2 medium shallots, minced

3 tablespoons butter

¼ cup honey

1 egg yolk

With a pair of poultry shears, cut the chicken in half lengthwise down the center of the backbone. Open it flat and press down with the heel of your hand to flatten the chicken as much as possible. Continue cutting through the center of the breast bone. Separate the halves and remove as many of the small rib bones as you can, using pliers if needed. Rinse the chicken and place both halves in a large plastic bag. Pour the wine, lemon juice and salt into the bag. Seal the bag, leaving a small opening at the end. Squeeze out as much air as you can and seal the bag completely. Refrigerate the chicken for 6 to 8 hours, or overnight, turning occasionally.

When ready to cook, preheat oven to 325°F. Remove the chicken from the bag and place the chicken, skin side up, in a shallow baking dish. Add the marinade to the baking dish and roast, uncovered, for 2 hours, basting occasionally with the pan juices.

When the chicken is cooked, transfer it to a serving platter and keep it warm. Set aside the pan juices. In a medium-size saucepan, briefly sauté the minced shallots in butter, being careful not to burn them. Add 2 cups of the reserved pan juices and reduce over high heat to about one cup (it will take 20 to 30 minutes to reduce). Watch carefully, as the juices will reduce more quickly and burn more easily toward the end. Remove from the heat and stir in the honey. In a small bowl, mix about 2 tablespoons of the hot lemon sauce with the egg yolk. Slowly stir in another 2 tablespoons of hot lemon sauce and then stir the egg mixture back into the remaining hot lemon sauce.

To serve, pour the sauce over the chicken and add a colorful garnish, such as a sprig of a fresh green herb and a twist of lemon.

Serves 6.

We are fortunate to have free-range chicken widely available in Sonoma County. The manner in which these chickens are raised makes such a wonderful difference in flavor and tenderness. If it is possible for you to substitute free-range for more conventionally raised chicken, I'm sure you'll agree it is worth the extra cost.

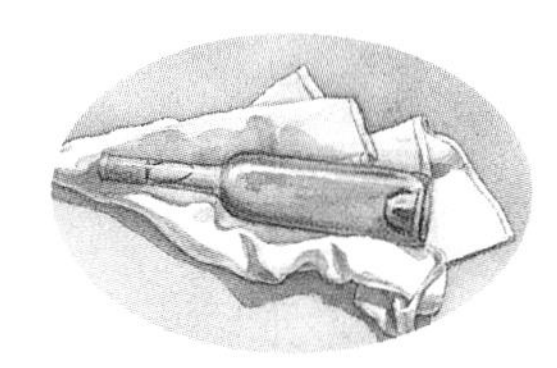

VIANSA WINE SUGGESTION

'Vittoria' Pinot Grigio, Sauvignon Blanc or Chardonnay

Squid Rings and Tentacles with Caper Sauce

CALAMARI CON SALSA DI CAPPERI

Squid Rings and Tentacles with Caper Sauce

3 pounds calamari (squid) bodies and tentacles, cleaned

2 cups unseasoned dried bread crumbs (about 10 slices white bread, if making your own dried crumbs)

2 tablespoons minced fresh thyme

2 teaspoons salt

½ teaspoon pepper

⅓ cup Viansa Extra Virgin Olive Oil

CAPER SAUCE

2 large garlic cloves, minced

¼ cup capers, minced

2 teaspoons minced fresh thyme

1 cup mayonnaise

¼ cup freshly squeezed lemon juice (about 2 lemons)

Even though calamari is usually sold as "cleaned," this usually means only skinned. You will still need to check each one to make sure the transparent backbone and fat have been removed. Remove tentacles from the bodies. If necessary, remove the head from the tentacles. Pinch or pop the beak from the mouth, which may remain attached to the tentacles. (For more detailed information on cleaning squid, see Fettuccine recipe on page 33).

Preheat oven to 450°F.

Rinse and cut calamari bodies into ½-inch rings. Pat the rings and tentacles dry with paper towels. (This is crucial so the breading does not become soggy.) In a large bowl, combine bread crumbs, thyme, salt and pepper. Toss the calamari pieces with crumb mixture (you may have some crumb mixture left over). Lightly oil a large baking sheet and spread the calamari evenly over it. Slowly and evenly drizzle the extra virgin olive oil over the top of the calamari. With 2 large flat spoons or spatulas, carefully toss calamari to coat evenly.

Bake for 20 minutes, or until calamari is golden brown and crunchy. Toss the calamari halfway through cooking so that it browns evenly. Serve immediately with sauce.

CAPER SAUCE

Combine sauce ingredients and mix well. If possible, allow the sauce to sit in the refrigerator for at least 30 minutes before serving to marry its flavors.

Serves 8.

Everyone loves fried calamari, especially my family. In fact, they love it so much that I decided to create a more healthful, lower fat version. Instead of deep-frying the calamari, I lightly drizzle the breaded calamari with a minimal amount of extra virgin olive oil and bake it. The results are deliciously similar!

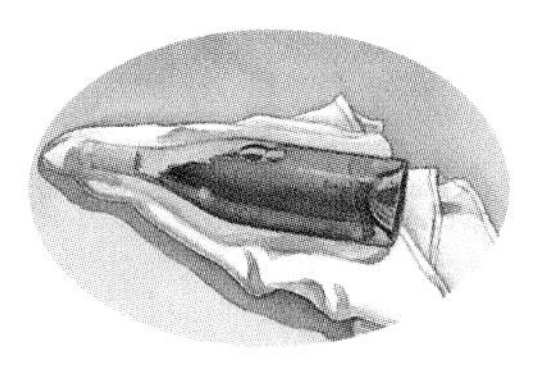

VIANSA WINE SUGGESTION

'Cento per Cento' Chardonnay, Reserve Chardonnay or Chardonnay

CALAMARI RIPIENI CON SALSA DI ANETO

Stuffed Squid with Dill Sauce

Calamari — or squid — is an Italian specialty that has become increasingly popular throughout the United States. I created this version of succulent stuffed squid bodies for our first Tuscan Club dinner at the winery. I remember being so concerned that it might be a stretch for some American palates — and being so pleased when everyone wolfed it down!

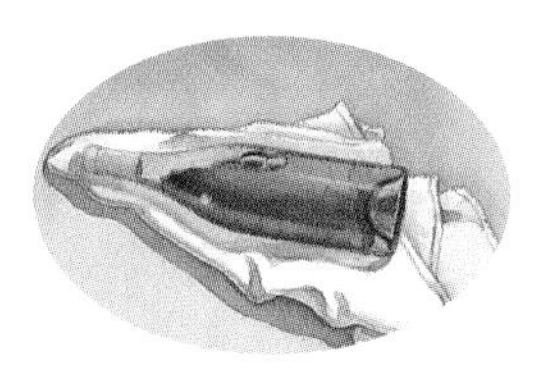

VIANSA WINE SUGGESTION
Chardonnay, 'Vittoria' Pinot Grigio or Sauvignon Blanc

2 slices stale white bread, crust removed

1 cup milk

2½ pounds large calamari (squid) bodies and tentacles, cleaned

1 cup minced onion

¾ cup minced red bell pepper

2 cloves garlic, minced

½ cup minced celery

2 tablespoons olive oil

2 tablespoons minced Italian parsley

½ teaspoon salt

¼ teaspoon pepper

24 toothpicks (approximately)

⅓ cup minced shallots

1 small tomato, peeled, seeded and diced

2 tablespoons minced fresh dill

¼ cup freshly squeezed lemon juice (about 2 lemons)

1 cup white wine

1 tablespoon flour

Fresh dill sprigs for garnish

Soak the bread in milk until soft. Separate the tentacles from the cleaned calamari. You should have about 24 bodies or sacs. If necessary, pinch or pop the beak from the mouth. (For more detailed information on cleaning squid, see Fettuccine recipe on page 33.) Finely dice the tentacles and set aside. In a medium-size skillet, sauté the onion, red bell pepper, garlic and celery in the olive oil for 10 minutes. Stir in the diced tentacles and sauté for an additional minute.

Preheat oven to 325°F.

Squeeze the milk from the bread, crumble and add to the sautéed vegetables, mixing well to combine. Add the minced parsley, salt and pepper. Using a small spoon or a pastry bag with a large tip, pipe the calamari sacs half-full of the vegetable mixture (this allows room for the stuffing to swell). Secure the open ends of the calamari with toothpicks.

Place the stuffed calamari in a lightly oiled, shallow 9x13-inch baking dish. Top with the minced shallots, tomato, 1 tablespoon of the minced dill, lemon juice and white wine. Cover and bake for 20 minutes. Remove from the oven, place the calamari on a heated platter and keep warm. Sprinkle 1 tablespoon flour into the cooking juices and stir over medium heat until juices thicken, about 5 minutes. Sprinkle the platter or individual plates with the remaining tablespoon of minced fresh dill. Arrange the cooked calamari on the dill-sprinkled platter or plates and top each calamari with a heaping teaspoon of the sauce. Serve hot, garnished with sprigs of fresh dill.

Serves 8 (3 calamari per person).

INSALATA DI MARE

Chilled Tuscan Squid, Octopus and Pepper Salad

SEAFOOD SALAD

2½ pounds calamari (squid), cleaned

1 pound baby octopus tentacles (optional)

½ red bell pepper, seeded, deveined and diced

½ yellow bell pepper, seeded, deveined and diced

¼ cup capers, rinsed and drained

½ cup minced fresh basil

2 tablespoons minced Italian parsley

VINAIGRETTE

3 cloves garlic, minced

2 tablespoons freshly squeezed lemon juice

2 tablespoons champagne or white wine vinegar

½ cup olive oil

½ teaspoon salt

¼ teaspoon pepper

Rinse the calamari bodies and tentacles and cut bodies into ½ inch rings. (For detailed cleaning directions, see Fettuccine recipe on page 33.) Cook the calamari rings and tentacles in boiling water for about 1 minute, until no longer translucent. Drain and cool. Cook the cleaned octopus in boiling water for 45 seconds, drain and cool.

In a large bowl, combine the calamari and octopus with the peppers, capers, basil and parsley. In a small bowl, whisk together the garlic, lemon juice, vinegar, olive oil, salt and pepper. Toss with seafood mixture, cover with plastic wrap and place in refrigerator to marinate, tossing occasionally, for 1 to 2 hours. If desired, serve in individual butter lettuce cups.

Serves 10 to 12 as an appetizer.

Markets usually sell cleaned calamari, with the thin purple skin, innards and head removed. Occasionally they miss a few, so check each body and make sure the thin, translucent backbone has been removed. Insert your finger in the cavity and the thin piece will slip out. Any small pieces of fat will come out as well. Baby octopus is sold without the bodies, so just make sure the tentacles are clean.

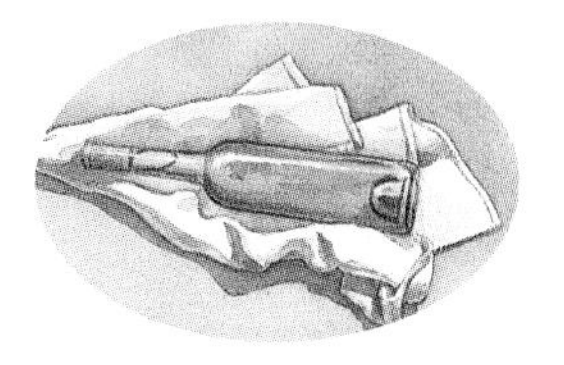

VIANSA WINE SUGGESTION
Sauvignon Blanc or Chardonnay

Crab Crepes with Avocado Sauce

CRESPELLE DI GRANCHIO CON SALSA DI AVOCADO

Crab Crepes with Avocado Sauce

CREPES
2 large eggs
1 teaspoon salt
1 tablespoon sugar
¼ cup Viansa Chardonnay
¾ cup flour
1¼ cups milk
¼ cup butter, melted

FILLING
½ cup mayonnaise
¼ teaspoon curry powder
2 tablespoons minced onion
2 cups fresh crab meat (about 12 ounces)
1 tablespoon freshly squeezed lemon juice
1 tablespoon Viansa Chardonnay
¼ cup minced roasted red bell peppers

AVOCADO SAUCE
2 packages (3 ounces each) cream cheese, softened
2 tablespoons freshly squeezed lemon juice
1 tablespoon Viansa Chardonnay
2 large avocados, peeled, pitted and mashed

CREPES

In a medium bowl, whisk eggs until frothy. Add salt, sugar and wine and whisk thoroughly. Add flour and milk alternately, beating well after each addition. Cover and allow the batter to rest one hour in the refrigerator. Whisk again to mix. Spread a very small amount of butter with a brush (or paper towel) on a 6 to 8-inch non-stick crepe pan or skillet. Pour 3 tablespoons batter into the center of the pan for each crepe (use a large cooking or serving spoon that holds three tablespoons, so you can pour the batter all at once). Quickly swirl to spread the batter to a 6-inch circle. Brown lightly on the underside over medium heat, turn to briefly brown the second side (use a rubber spatula to loosen the crepe around the edges, slide it under and flip the crepe over). Slide each crepe onto waxed paper. Crepes can be stacked on waxed paper liners until ready for use. If preparing well ahead of time, wrap the stack of crepes in plastic wrap and refrigerate.

Makes 12 to 14 crepes.

FILLING

In a small bowl, combine all the filling ingredients.

Spread 2 to 3 tablespoons filling on the side of the crepe that was cooked last (the first side usually looks the best, so use it as the outside). Roll up crepes to hold filling. Transfer filled crepes to a serving platter. If possible, heat filled crepes at 325°F for 10 to 15 minutes before serving.

AVOCADO SAUCE

Beat together the cream cheese, lemon juice and Chardonnay until smooth and creamy. Stir in avocado. Spoon 2 to 3 tablespoons sauce over top of each warm crepe.

Serves 6.

This versatile crepe is a favorite of mine for bridal and baby showers or other light luncheons. Since it does not have to be served hot, it is a good choice for a buffet or similar meal where keeping food hot is difficult.

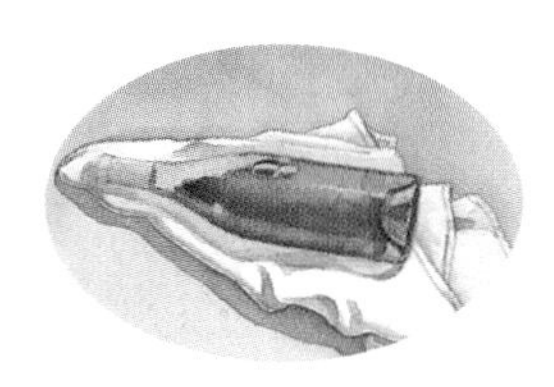

VIANSA WINE SUGGESTION
Reserve Chardonnay, Chardonnay or 'Imbianco' Barbera Rosé

SPIEDINI DI GAMBERONI E CAPESANTI

Prawn and Scallop Skewers

Because Italy is surrounded by the sea, fish make up an important part of the Italian diet. As you travel from province to province you may encounter a different name for the same dish, or the same name for a different dish — it can be very frustrating! A perfect example is scampi. It can be a prawn from the Adriatic, a salt water crayfish, or a Dublin Bay prawn. Gamberoni or gamberi or gamberetti can be a shrimp or a prawn. It can be very confusing, and the only sure way to know is to actually see it!

I have chosen to call my large prawns gamberoni.

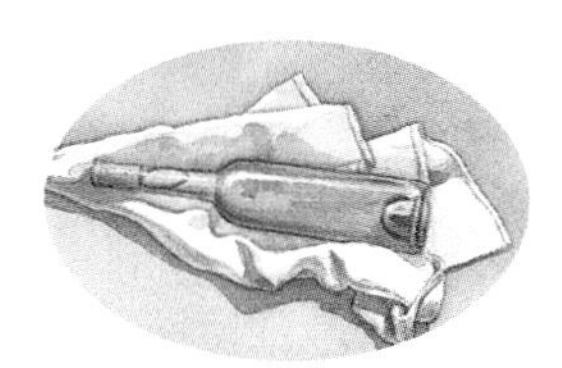

VIANSA WINE SUGGESTION
Sauvignon Blanc, Chardonnay or Nebbiolo

12 wooden skewers (10 to 12 inches long)

2 dozen large prawns, shelled and deveined

2 dozen sea scallops

¾ cup minced Italian parsley

¾ cup minced watercress

1 cup unseasoned dried bread crumbs

1 tablespoon minced or mashed garlic

¼ teaspoon pepper

½ to ⅔ cup olive oil

2 lemons, cut into wedges (to use for garnish)

Rub the skewers against each other on all surfaces to remove any splinters. Immerse skewers in cold water and allow to soak.

Rinse the prawns and scallops under cold, running water. Pat dry with paper towels.

In a large bowl, combine the parsley, watercress, bread crumbs, garlic and pepper and mix together thoroughly. Dunk each prawn and scallop into the olive oil, then coat with the herb breading. Thread two prawns and two scallops, alternately, onto each skewer. Use leftover crumb mixture to pat onto prawns and scallops where necessary.

Position the oven rack 6 to 8 inches under the broiler. Broil the skewered shellfish about 2 to 3 minutes on each side, or until very lightly browned. Serve with lemon wedges.

Serves 6.

CACCIUCCO

Tuscan Seafood Soup

- 3 tablespoons olive oil
- 3 tablespoons butter
- 1 large yellow onion, chopped
- 1 red or yellow bell pepper, chopped
- 2 cloves garlic, minced
- 1 carrot, peeled and chopped
- 3 large tomatoes, peeled and chopped
- 2 cups chicken broth
- 1 cup dry white wine
- ½ teaspoon salt
- ½ teaspoon paprika
- 1 teaspoon sugar
- 1½ pounds fresh ling cod, halibut, turbot or shark
- 1 pound medium prawns, shelled and deveined
- 1 tablespoon minced fresh basil
- 3 tablespoons minced Italian parsley

In a 6-quart pot, melt the butter in the olive oil. Sauté the onion and pepper over medium heat, 8 to 10 minutes. Add the garlic, carrot, tomatoes, chicken broth, wine, salt, paprika and sugar. Bring mixture to a boil, then reduce the heat and simmer for 15 minutes. Bone the fish if necessary and cut it into 1-inch cubes. Add the fish to the pot and simmer for 5 minutes. Add the prawns and the basil and cook an additional 3 to 4 minutes, until the prawns are firm and pink.

Ladle stew into a soup tureen or deep serving bowl. Sprinkle with fresh parsley.

Serves 6.

Cacciucco is a delicious seafood stew created in Livorno and made famous in San Francisco's North Beach. This recipe is flexible; substitute your favorite seafood for the ones I've specified. Try the Cacciucco served over rice, accompanied by fresh coleslaw or sliced tomatoes and marinated cucumbers.

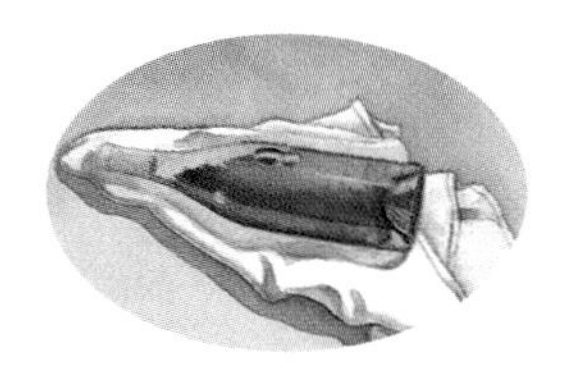

VIANSA WINE SUGGESTION
Chardonnay or
'Riserva Anatra Bianco' Trebbiano

Verdura e Insalata

Vegetables and Salad

Each summer, our garden yields the most magnificent array of vegetables—

plump, sweet tomatoes, crisp greens, tender squashes and fresh herbs.

We enjoy this abundance in many ways—

grilled, steamed, sautéed or in a colorful assortment of salads.

What a delight it is to taste the earth's bounty!

The River Sérchio flows gently past the ancient walled city of Lucca.

RADICCHIO AL FORNO

Roasted Radicchio

The long, slow baking of this bitter lettuce results in a succulent, tender and sweet vegetable. It's a perfect accompaniment to a pasta dish, roasted chicken or pork.

If the radicchio is particularly large, one quarter of a head per person would probably be enough—especially if it is accompanying a large meal.

2 heads radicchio

3 tablespoons Viansa Extra Virgin Olive Oil

½ teaspoon salt

8 twists freshly ground black pepper

Preheat oven to 350°F.

Cut radicchio lengthwise into quarters. Place the wedges in a shallow baking dish and drizzle each with about 1 teaspoon olive oil. Sprinkle with salt and freshly ground pepper.

Bake, uncovered, for 1 hour, until crisp. Serve immediately.

Serves 4 (2 wedges each).

GONDOLE DI ZUCCA CON SPINACI, PANCETTA E FORMAGGIO

Zucchini Gondolas with Spinach, Bacon and Cheese

8 small zucchini

8 slices bacon

⅓ cup minced white onion

1 bunch fresh spinach, cleaned and chopped (or one 10-ounce package frozen chopped spinach, thawed)

1 tablespoon minced fresh basil

2 tablespoons flour

¼ cup milk

1 teaspoon salt

¼ teaspoon pepper

½ cup grated sharp cheddar cheese

Preheat oven to 350°F.

Carefully trim stems from the zucchini. Bring a large pot of water to a boil, immerse the zucchini and reduce heat. Simmer zucchini until barely tender when gently pierced with a fork, approximately 8 to 10 minutes. Drain and cool slightly. Cut ⅓ off the top of each zucchini (lengthwise). Carefully hollow out the center of each zucchini, using a melon baller or a sharp paring knife and a small spoon (be careful not to break through the shells). Leave a shell ¼-inch to ½-inch thick. Place the shells, cut side down, on paper towels to drain. Dice the zucchini pulp.

In a large skillet, sauté the bacon until crisp. Remove bacon and drain on paper towels to remove excess grease. Crumble bacon into small pieces and set aside. Pour off all but 1 tablespoon of the drippings. Return the skillet to the heat and sauté the minced onion for 2 to 3 minutes, then lower heat and add diced zucchini, spinach and basil. Cook until spinach wilts. Blend together flour and milk in a small bowl, and then stir into spinach mixture. Add salt and pepper. Cook over low heat, stirring, until thickened. Place the zucchini shells in a shallow baking dish. Carefully spoon the spinach mixture into the shells and top with grated cheese and crumbled bacon.

Bake for 15 to 20 minutes, until the zucchini shells are hot and the cheese has melted.

Serves 8.

Spinach is probably the most popular vegetable in Tuscany—next to zucchini! In the produce section of Tuscan supermarkets they even sell spinach cooked and formed into balls the size of grapefruit! Spinach is usually served plain along with meat for the main course, or tucked into frittatas, pies or various antipasti dishes. This recipe could be adapted to almost any course of your meal.

Roasted Vegetables with Fresh Herbs

VERDURE MISTE ARROSTITE ALLE ERBE

Roasted Vegetables with Fresh Herbs

1 red onion, peeled and cut into 6 wedges

3 leeks, white parts only, rinsed and cut in half crosswise, and then in half lengthwise

1 fennel bulb, trimmed and cut into 8 wedges

1 pound red potatoes, cut into 1½-inch pieces

1 pound sweet potatoes, peeled and cut into 1½-inch pieces

¾ pound carrots, peeled and cut into 1½-inch lengths

1½ pounds banana squash, butternut squash or pumpkin, peeled, seeded and cut into 1½-inch cubes

30 cloves "stovetop roasted" garlic (see sidebar and directions)

1 cup Viansa Extra VIrgin Olive Oil

1 tablespoon salt

1 teaspoon pepper

30 sprigs fresh thyme

4 sprigs fresh rosemary, about 6 inches each

40 leaves fresh sage

Preheat oven to 425°F.

Combine all of the vegetables and the roasted garlic in a large bowl. Add oil, salt and pepper and toss well to combine. Strip the leaves off the sprigs of thyme and rosemary and add to the vegetables, along with the sage leaves. Toss again and then spread vegetables evenly in a large, shallow roasting pan. Roast for 35 to 45 minutes, until all the vegetables are tender when pierced with a fork.

Serves 8 to 10.

"Stovetop Roasted Garlic"

Immerse peeled garlic cloves in boiling water for 3 minutes. Drain and pat dry with paper towels. In a small, heavy saucepan or skillet, heat 1 cup olive oil and add as many cloves as you like (the oil should cover at least half the cloves). Cook the garlic cloves over medium-high heat for about 7 minutes, turning continuously, until brown. Remove the garlic cloves and drain on paper towels. Cool garlic oil and reserve for other uses such as salad dressings or sautéing vegetables or chicken.

We use so much roasted garlic that I developed a speedy method to obtain the same sweet, delicious results as baking the whole heads. These "stovetop roasted" garlic cloves keep well in the refrigerator, so make a large batch to have "roasted" garlic available when needed. It is especially easy to make, since many markets now sell peeled garlic!

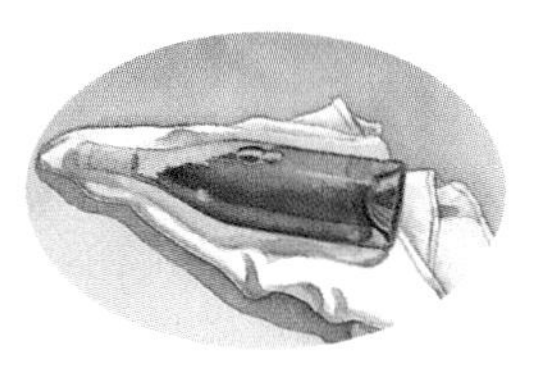

VIANSA WINE SUGGESTION

Chardonnay or 'Piccolo Toscano' Sangiovese

LATTUGA RIPIENA ALLA TOSCANA

Tuscan Stuffed Lettuce

I risked making enemies with several of our special event cooks when I served these tasty little packets at our first Tuscan Club dinner. They made almost 500 of them and it was pretty tough to put them on any kind of small assembly work for a while after that! In the end, though, all agreed it was worth it. The combined taste of these flavorful ingredients drew raves from our guests!

2 heads butter lettuce

2 tablespoons olive oil

4 large cloves garlic, minced

12 kalamata olives, pitted and coarsely chopped

3 tablespoons golden raisins

¼ cup pine nuts

¼ cup fontina cheese, diced (approximately 1½ ounces)

2 tablespoons freshly grated Romano cheese

Separate leaves of lettuce, select 12 fresh large outer leaves and rinse. (You may not need 12 leaves, but this gives you a few extra in case you have excess filling or one tears while preparing it.) Cut out the core section from the base of each leaf and, one at a time, plunge leaves into boiling water for about 10 seconds. Remove and drain on paper towels (they can be stacked with paper towels between the leaves).

Preheat oven to 350°F.

Sauté garlic in olive oil over very low heat until it starts to turn light brown. Transfer garlic to a small bowl and reserve oil.

Combine the chopped olives, raisins, pine nuts, fontina and 1 tablespoon of the grated Romano cheese and mix together with the garlic. Place 1 to 2 tablespoons of filling in the center of each leaf (adjust the amount of filling if leaves are small). Gently wrap each leaf around the filling and place the rolls, seam side down, on an oiled baking sheet. Brush tops with reserved garlic oil and sprinkle with remaining Romano cheese. Bake for 10 minutes. Remove to serving platter and serve hot.

Serves 8 (1 large or 2 small stuffed leaves per person).

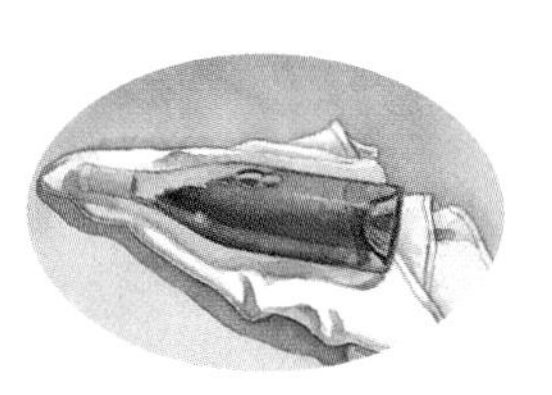

VIANSA WINE SUGGESTION
Chardonnay or Sauvignon Blanc

POMODORI ROMA AL FORNO

Baked Roma Tomatoes

12 Roma tomatoes

2 tablespoons Viansa Extra Virgin Olive Oil

Kosher salt

Freshly ground black pepper

Preheat oven to 300°F.

Carefully cut out the small core at the stem end of each tomato and slice the tomato in half lengthwise. Arrange tomatoes, cut side up, in a shallow baking pan and brush or spoon about ¼ teaspoon of oil on each tomato half and sprinkle with a pinch of salt and freshly ground pepper.

Bake for approximately 1 to 1½ hours, depending on the size of the tomatoes. The tomatoes should appear shriveled, but not entirely flattened and dried out.

Serves 8 (3 tomato halves per person).

(See photograph on page 68 with Lemon Roasted Chicken with Lemon-Honey Sauce.)

Naturally, Roma tomatoes picked ripe from your garden provide the very best flavor! However, community gardens, farmers markets and gourmet produce markets provide equally good sources for vine-fresh tomatoes. Bring the tomatoes to the peak of ripeness on your kitchen counter. The only time they need to be refrigerated is when they are completely ripe and you need to store them for a day or so before use.

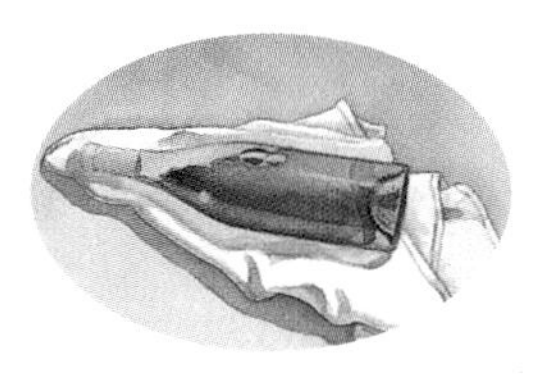

VIANSA WINE SUGGESTION

'Riserva Anatra Bianco' Trebbiano

ZUCCHINI RIPIENI FREDDI

Chilled Zucchini with Avocado and Chives

This is a great dish to supplement a summer buffet. The chilled and stuffed zucchini may be enjoyed as an appetizer, a salad or as a side dish with an "al fresco" lunch or dinner.

4 medium yellow or green zucchini

3 ripe avocados, chilled, pitted and peeled

2 tablespoons minced fresh basil

3 tablespoons minced fresh chives

1 teaspoon garlic salt

¼ teaspoon white pepper

1 tablespoon freshly squeezed lemon juice

1 tablespoon dry white wine

2 dashes Tabasco sauce

Steam or boil whole zucchini until barely tender, 12 to 15 minutes. Remove from pan and chill about 1 hour. When chilled, slice the zucchini in half lengthwise and carefully hollow out the center, using a melon baller or a sharp paring knife and small spoon. Leave a shell about ¼ to ½-inch thick. Place the shells cut side down on a paper towel to drain, and chill until ready to use.

Purée the remaining ingredients and, using a pastry tube, pipe filling down the center of each zucchini cavity. A spoon can also be used to spoon filling into zucchini cavities. Serve cold.

Serves 8.

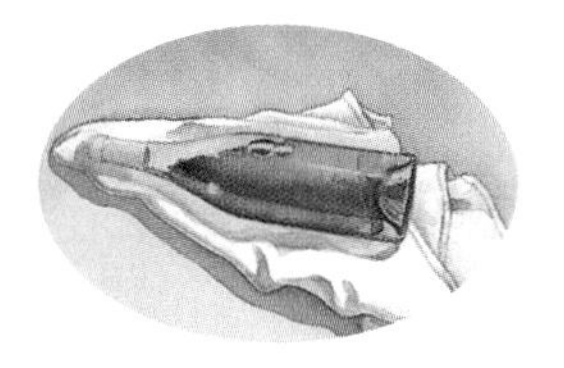

VIANSA WINE SUGGESTION

Chardonnay, Sauvignon Blanc or 'Imbianco' Barbera Rosé

VERDURE ALLA BRACE CON FORMAGGIO DI CAPRA

Grilled Vegetables with Goat Cheese and Tomato Dressing

GRILLED VEGETABLES

1 large eggplant (about 1½ pounds)

Salt

6 medium yellow or green zucchini (about 1½ pounds)

1 large red onion, peeled

2 yellow bell peppers

⅓ to ½ cup olive oil

3 tablespoons minced fresh Italian herbs (basil, thyme, oregano, tarragon or a mixture)

Freshly ground black pepper (about 10 twists of the grinder)

8 ounces goat cheese

2 tablespoons minced Italian parsley

TOMATO DRESSING

6 to 8 cherry tomatoes (or, if possible, 10 to 12 Sweet 100 cherry tomatoes)

2 tablespoons freshly squeezed lemon juice

½ cup Viansa Extra Virgin Olive Oil

1 tablespoon minced fresh tarragon

¼ teaspoon salt

GRILLED VEGETABLES

Trim eggplant and slice into ½-inch thick rings (it is not necessary to peel the eggplant). Sprinkle eggplant slices moderately with salt and allow to sit for 1 to 2 hours in a colander to release their moisture and bitterness. (If time is critical, steam over rapidly boiling water for 3 to 4 minutes.) Rinse gently and squeeze out moisture thoroughly for best cooking results.

Trim and slice zucchini lengthwise into ½-inch thick slices.

Trim and slice onion into ¼-inch thick slices.

Roast the yellow peppers over a flame (or under the broiler) until charred on all sides. Place in a paper bag for 15 minutes to steam, and then peel off the skin, discard membranes and seeds, and cut into strips ½-inch wide.

Stir the Italian herbs, ½ teaspoon salt and pepper into the olive oil and brush onto both sides of the eggplant, zucchini and onion slices.

Light a grill and when the coals are hot, spread them into a single layer and position the rack at least 4 inches from the coals. Place the vegetables on the grill over medium heat and cook until tender and lightly browned on both sides, about 8 to 12 minutes. Baste as necessary, watching carefully so they don't burn.

Arrange eggplant and zucchini slices on a large, flat platter. Separate the onion rings and scatter over eggplant and zucchini. Place yellow pepper slices on top, crumble the goat cheese over the vegetables and sprinkle the parsley over all. Serve immediately, or refrigerate and chill for an hour or so. Serve grilled vegetable platter, hot or cold, with tomato dressing on the side.

TOMATO DRESSING

Purée cherry tomatoes in a food processor or blender and mix well with remaining ingredients.

Serves 8.

This versatile vegetable dish can be served chilled as a hearty salad, at room temperature—or even hot with the dressing at room temperature. Feel free to replace any of the vegetables with whatever is fresh and in season. To purchase eggplant with the fewest seeds, weigh two eggplants that appear to be the same size. The lighter eggplant has fewer seeds.

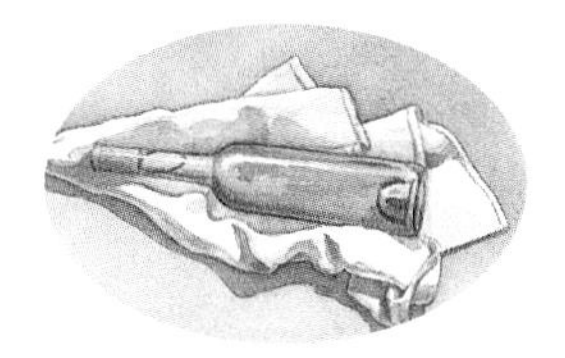

VIANSA WINE SUGGESTION

Sauvignon Blanc or 'Riserva Anatra Bianco' Trebbiano

The Marketplace Torta Rustica

TORTA RUSTICA ALLA MERCATO

The Marketplace Torta Rustica

CRUST
4 cups all-purpose flour
1 teaspoon salt
1 cup cold unsalted butter (2 sticks), cut into pieces
2 eggs
2 egg yolks
⅓ cup milk

TORTA FILLING
¼ cup olive oil
2 medium leeks (white parts only), thinly sliced
1 large bulb fennel, trimmed and coarsely chopped
2 teaspoons fennel seed
2 packages (10 ounces each) frozen chopped spinach, thawed and squeezed dry
1 cup ricotta cheese
1 egg, beaten
¼ teaspoon salt
⅛ teaspoon pepper
⅓ cup freshly grated Parmesan cheese
⅓ cup grated mozzarella cheese
1 red bell pepper, roasted, skinned, seeded, deveined and cut into thin strips
5 ounces fontina cheese, thinly sliced
1 egg yolk (to brush on crust)

CRUST

Mix flour, salt and butter in a food processor or electric mixer until the mixture resembles coarse cornmeal. Beat the eggs, egg yolks and milk together, then add to processor. Mix just until dough forms a ball. Wrap the dough tightly in plastic wrap and let it rest for 30 minutes in the refrigerator.

TORTA FILLING

Sauté leeks, fennel and fennel seed in olive oil until limp; set aside and cool to room temperature. In a separate bowl, mix together the spinach, ricotta, egg, salt and pepper; set aside. Combine the grated cheeses in a small bowl and set aside.

Preheat oven to 375°F.

On a floured surface, roll out approximately ¾ of the dough into a 14 to 15-inch circle about ⅛-inch thick. Carefully place the dough into an 8 to 9-inch springform pan, making sure the dough covers sides of pan and hangs over top at least ½-inch. Layer the ingredients in the crust by spreading half the spinach mixture, half the red pepper strips, half the grated cheese, half the fontina slices and half the leek and fennel mixture. Repeat the layers using the remaining ingredients.

Roll out remaining dough to the size of the top of the torta, including a ½-inch overlap, and place on top of the filled torta. Fold the dough from the bottom crust over the top and crimp the edges together, creating a lip. Use any leftover dough to make a design on the top, if desired. Lightly beat the egg yolk and brush the top of the torta. Bake for about 1 hour, or until golden brown. Let cool, then cut into wedges. Serve warm or cold. If taking on a picnic, leave side rim of the springform pan on while transporting and remove it to serve the torta.

Serves 10 to 12.

Different regions, villages and even households each have their favorite combination of layers surrounded by a savory crust—their very own version of Torta Rustica. A flavorful favorite of Viansa visitors since we opened, this is my own creation. Sometimes I add grilled eggplant (as in the accompanying photo), zucchini, portobello mushrooms or thin slices of salami. A springform pan with removable sides is essential for this recipe.

VIANSA WINE SUGGESTION
'Di Pacomio' Aleatico, Sauvignon Blanc or 'Imbianco' Barbera Rosé

TORTA DI RISO CON ZUCCHINI E PANCETTA

Rice Cake with Zucchini and Bacon

An Italian torta is essentially a cake, in the sense of not having a crust or shell which would then make it a pie. It can be—and often is—a combination of just about anything, sweet or savory.

CRUST
1¼ cups flour
½ teaspoon salt
½ teaspoon crushed fennel seed
½ cup butter (1 stick), at room temperature
½ cup grated cheddar cheese, at room temperature

FILLING
8 slices bacon
2 cups thinly sliced zucchini
½ cup minced yellow or white onion
2 large cloves garlic, minced
6 eggs
1 cup sour cream
1 teaspoon salt
2 cups cooked rice
1 cup grated cheddar cheese

CRUST

Using a food processor or mixing by hand in a large bowl, combine the salt and fennel seed with the flour. Add the butter and cheese and work into flour, mixing well until the dough forms a solid ball. Press dough in an even layer on the bottom and one inch up the sides of an 8 to 9-inch springform pan.

FILLING

In a large skillet, sauté the bacon until crisp. Remove bacon and drain on paper towels to remove excess grease. Crumble bacon into small pieces and set aside. Pour off all but 2 tablespoons of the drippings and return skillet to heat. Add zucchini, onion and garlic and cook over medium heat until tender (about 10 minutes), stirring occasionally. Remove zucchini mixture from skillet and allow to cool.

Preheat oven to 350°F.

Beat eggs in a large bowl. Add sour cream, salt, cooked rice, cheese, sautéed zucchini mixture and crumbled bacon. Mix well and pour the mixture into the pastry shell. Smooth the top with a flat spatula and bake 55 minutes, or until golden brown and set (a knife inserted in the center comes out clean). Let stand at least 15 minutes, then loosen the edges by running a knife between the crust and the pan, and remove sides of the pan. Cut into wedges and serve warm or cold. If taking on a picnic, leave side rim of the springform pan on while transporting and remove it to serve.

Serves 12.

VIANSA WINE SUGGESTION
'Athena' Dolcetto, Chardonnay or 'Imbianco' Barbera Rosé

FRITELLE DI GRANTURCO

Corn Griddle Cakes

3 cups milk

1 cup polenta or corn meal

3 cups fresh yellow corn kernels (about 4 medium ears)

1 cup flour

2 teaspoons baking powder

¼ cup minced fresh basil

2 tablespoons thinly sliced green onions

2 teaspoons salt

⅛ teaspoon freshly ground pepper

6 egg whites

Olive oil

❧Warm the milk in a large saucepan over medium-low heat and slowly drizzle in the polenta, stirring to incorporate. Cook over low heat for 3 to 4 minutes, stirring constantly, just until the milk is absorbed. Transfer polenta to a large bowl and cool for 30 minutes. Meanwhile, plunge corn kernels into boiling water for 2 to 3 minutes and drain.

❧Add the flour, baking powder, basil, green onions, salt, pepper and blanched corn to the cooled polenta and mix together thoroughly. In a separate bowl, beat the egg whites into firm peaks and fold gently into the corn mixture.

❧Heat a large non-stick skillet and brush lightly with olive oil. Drop about 3 tablespoons of corn mixture onto hot surface, forming small cakes about 3 inches across. (Try to be consistent; it looks better if all the cakes are about the same size.) Cook about 1 minute, until the underside is golden brown. Turn and brown the second side. Brush more oil on skillet if needed. Place the cooked corn cakes on paper towels, and reheat in a warm oven if necessary.

Makes about 3 dozen cakes.

Historically, corn has been one of the prime staples of both Italy and California. The early inhabitants of coastal Sonoma County, the Miwok Indians, used corn for many life-sustaining purposes. Both Italian and California cuisine use corn with an amazing variety of delicious results. For a savory midsummer alternative to corn on the cob, I often prepare this family favorite using polenta and fresh corn.

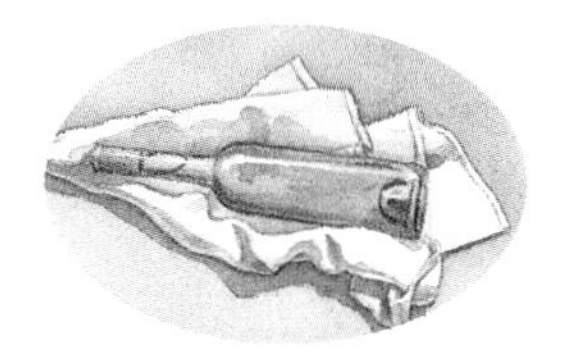

VIANSA WINE SUGGESTION
Sauvignon Blanc or 'Riserva Anatra Bianco' Trebbiano

Pasta Shells with Langostinos, Peas and Artichokes

PASTA DI GAMBERETTI CON VERDURE

Pasta Shells with Langostinos, Peas and Artichokes

PASTA SALAD

1 pound medium-size dried pasta shells

1 tablespoon olive oil

1 package (10 ounces) frozen peas

2 packages (9 ounces each) frozen artichoke hearts, cut in half

1½ pounds cooked langostinos or large bay shrimp

¼ cup minced fresh dill

DRESSING

1 clove garlic, minced

½ teaspoon salt

¼ teaspoon white pepper

⅓ cup Viansa Extra Virgin Olive Oil

1 tablespoon freshly squeezed lemon juice

1 tablespoon white wine vinegar

½ cup mayonnaise

2 teaspoons Viansa Hot Sweet Mustard

2 tablespoons freshly grated Romano cheese

PASTA SALAD

Cook pasta shells in a large pot of boiling salted water according to package directions. Drain in a large colander, rinse under cold running water for a few minutes to stop the cooking, and drain again. Toss pasta with oil. Cook peas and artichokes according to package directions, being careful not to overcook. Drain well. Combine peas, artichoke hearts, langostinos and dill with the pasta shells and toss to combine.

DRESSING

Combine dressing ingredients in a small bowl and whisk until smooth. Drizzle dressing over pasta mixture and gently toss to combine. Cover with plastic wrap and chill until ready to serve.

Serves 8.

When preparing this dish we love to include langostinos, which are tiny crawfish tails that are frequently stocked in our markets. However, if you are unable to locate them, small cooked bay shrimp work just fine.

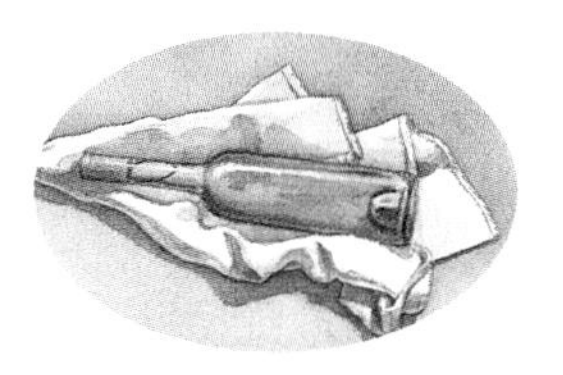

VIANSA WINE SUGGESTION
Sauvignon Blanc or Chardonnay

INSALATA ASSORTITE DI FAGIOLI

Deli Salad with Beans

Antipasti Misti, or Antipasti Assortiti, is on virtually every menu in Italy. The popularity of processed, brined or otherwise cooked "specialty" meats is incredible! They are usually eaten before a meal to keep the diners happy while the pasta is cooking, but deli meats are also found in a multitude of other dishes.

Americans aren't far behind, with 99% of them enjoying deli meats in sandwiches. I have taken this obsession a step further in the interest of health, and added a variety of other tasty (and nutritious) ingredients. Our friends, family and customers love it!

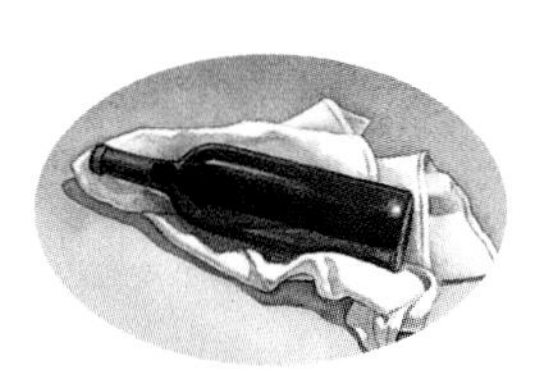

VIANSA WINE SUGGESTION
Nebbiolo or Sauvignon Blanc

SPICY BEANS

1 cup dried pink, cranberry or pinto beans (½ pound)

1 cup dried black beans (½ pound)

2 sprigs fresh thyme

6 cloves garlic, minced

1 large yellow onion, chopped

VINAIGRETTE

3 tablespoons Viansa Balsamic Vinegar

½ cup Viansa Extra Virgin Olive Oil

1 teaspoon minced garlic

1 teaspoon salt

½ teaspoon pepper

Dash of Tabasco sauce

CONDIMENTS

½ red bell pepper, cored, seeded and diced

½ cup chopped sweet pickles

1 large red onion, diced

2 cups cubed fontina cheese (about ½ pound)

½ cup chopped Italian parsley

3 cups assorted chopped deli meat, such as cooked ham, turkey, salami, sausage, mortadella or prosciutto

SPICY BEANS

Rinse the beans and soak them in warm water to cover for 30 minutes. Drain the beans, place them in a large saucepan and cover with fresh cold water. Add the thyme sprigs, garlic cloves and chopped onion. Bring to a boil then simmer over medium heat, covered, until tender but not mushy, about 50 to 60 minutes. Add more water, if necessary, to keep the beans submerged. Remove the thyme sprigs, drain the beans and transfer to a large bowl.

VINAIGRETTE

Whisk together the vinaigrette ingredients in a small bowl, then toss well with the warm beans. Cover beans with plastic wrap and refrigerate for an hour or so, until cool.

CONDIMENTS

After the beans have cooled, add the condiments and mix well.

Serves 10 to 12.

RUOTA DI PASTA AL POLLO AFFUMICATO

Wagon Wheel Pasta Salad with Smoked Chicken

PASTA AND CHICKEN

½ pound dried wagon wheel pasta

2 tablespoons olive oil

1 smoked chicken (about 3 pounds)

1 cup thinly sliced red onion

1 cup sliced green onions

1 cup thinly sliced celery

½ cup golden raisins

½ cup chopped pecans

DRESSING

1 cup sour cream

1 cup mayonnaise

¼ cup milk

1 tablespoon curry powder

2 tablespoons Viansa Balsamic Mustard

1 teaspoon salt

½ teaspoon white pepper

PASTA AND CHICKEN

Cook wagon wheels in a large pot of boiling salted water according to package directions. Drain in a large colander, rinse under cold running water for a few minutes to stop the cooking, and drain again. Toss the pasta with the olive oil in a large bowl, cover and set aside. Remove skin and bones from the chicken and shred the meat into bite-size pieces. Add the chicken, onions, celery, raisins and pecans to the pasta and toss to combine.

DRESSING

Whisk together dressing ingredients in a small bowl. Add dressing to pasta mixture and toss to combine. Cover with plastic wrap and chill until ready to serve.

Serves 8 to 10.

First developed for a large hillside party, this flavorful combination of smoked chicken, pasta, green onions and nuts with a hint of curry has become a popular picnic item in our Italian Marketplace. The novel pasta shape is reminiscent of a wagon wheel, with its circular shape and spokes in the center.

The smoked chicken can be replaced with two to three cups of another cooked meat, such as salami, sausage, ham, grilled chicken or lamb, if you prefer. If you have no Viansa Balsamic Mustard, substitute a country-style or sweet mustard instead.

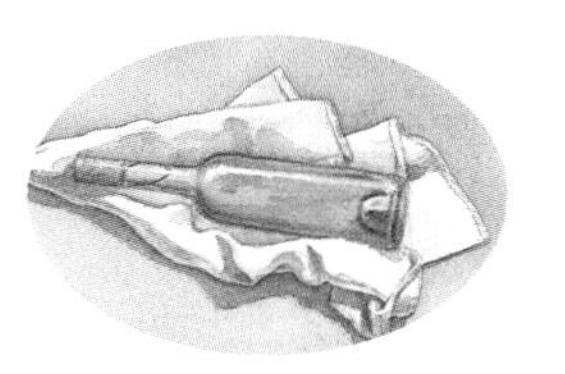

VIANSA WINE SUGGESTION

'Imbianco' Barbera Rosé, 'Athena' Dolcetto or Chardonnay

CONDIMENTO FAMOSO AL SAM

Sam's Creamy Gorgonzola-Balsamic Dressing

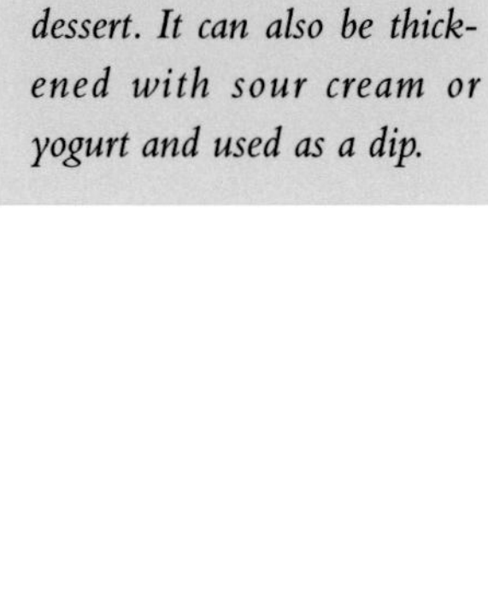

Sam, in his inimitable style, loves to don his apron and keep me company in the kitchen. Experimentation with some of his favorite flavors eventually led to this delicious salad dressing! This dressing is also terrific drizzled over poached chicken or sea bass. Or spoon the warm sauce over slices of lightly sautéed pears or apples for dessert. It can also be thickened with sour cream or yogurt and used as a dip.

4 ounces Gorgonzola cheese

1 tablespoon honey

2 tablespoons Viansa Balsamic Vinegar

Combine Gorgonzola, honey and balsamic vinegar in a small saucepan. Over very low heat, carefully melt cheese, stirring and mashing it as it melts. Once all the cheese has melted, remove it from the heat (mixture should be thick and creamy). Cool and toss with fresh greens of your choice. Extra dressing should be stored in the refrigerator.

Makes ¾ cup.

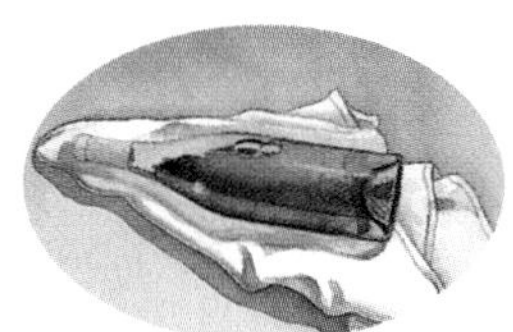

VIANSA WINE SUGGESTION
Reserve Chardonnay

INSALATA DI PASTA CON SPINACI, NOCI E ASIAGO

Asiago, Spinach and Toasted Walnuts with Fusilli

FUSILLI SALAD

2 cups chopped walnuts, toasted

1 pound fusilli pasta (corkscrew-shaped)

1 tablespoon olive oil

2 cups grated Asiago cheese

1 bunch green onions, sliced about ¼-inch thick

1 bunch fresh spinach, rinsed, drained and sliced into ½-inch wide ribbons

2 red bell peppers, deveined, seeded and cut into matchstick-size pieces

DRESSING

¾ cup Viansa Basil, Sun-Dried Tomato or Red Pepper Aioli

2 tablespoons Viansa Blood Orange Vinegar or white wine vinegar

2 tablespoons walnut oil

1½ teaspoons salt

1 teaspoon sugar

¼ teaspoon white pepper

FUSILLI SALAD

To toast walnuts, bake in oven at 300°F for 20 minutes, until light brown. Set toasted nuts aside.

Cook the fusilli in a large pot of boiling salted water according to package directions. Drain in a large colander, rinse under cold running water for a few minutes to stop the cooking, and drain again. Transfer fusilli to a large bowl and toss with the olive oil to prevent sticking.

DRESSING

Combine dressing ingredients in a small bowl and whisk until smooth.

To serve, toss the cheese, vegetables and toasted nuts with the pasta. Add the dressing and mix thoroughly. Cover with plastic wrap and chill until ready to serve.

Serves 12.

We use one of our aiolis (flavored mayonnaises) in this popular Marketplace salad. If you don't have any on hand, substitute the following: slightly less than ¾ cup mayonnaise mixed with 1 to 2 tablespoons of basil pesto or a flavorful mustard or relish or even minced fresh garlic and herbs.

When making pasta salads, I always toss the cooked, drained pasta with olive oil to prevent it from sticking together while I prepare the remaining ingredients.

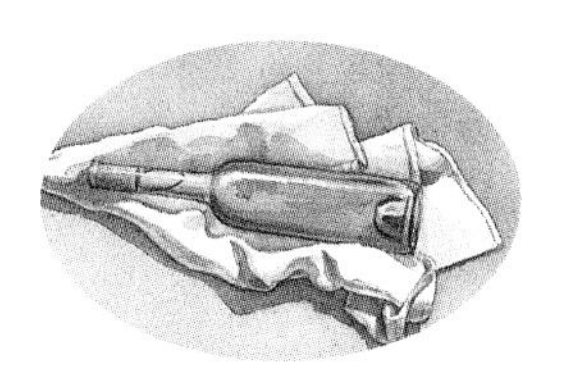

VIANSA WINE SUGGESTION

Sauvignon Blanc or 'Imbianco' Barbera Rosé

Spinach and Watercress Salad with Baked Goat Cheese

INSALATA DI SPINACI CON CAPRINO AL FORNO

Spinach and Watercress Salad with Baked Goat Cheese

CHEESE

¼ cup olive oil

10 to 12 ounces fresh goat cheese or Gorgonzola cheese, cut into 8 equal pieces about ½-inch thick

½ cup fine dried bread crumbs

2 teaspoons dried Italian seasoning

GREENS

1 small bunch spinach, stems removed

1 bunch watercress, thick stems removed

VINAIGRETTE

½ cup olive oil

2 tablespoons freshly squeezed lemon juice

2 tablespoons dry red wine

2 teaspoons Viansa Hot Sweet Mustard

¼ teaspoon salt

Freshly ground pepper to taste

CHEESE

❧Pour olive oil into a small bowl. Soak cheese in olive oil for about 5 minutes on each side to thoroughly coat. Combine bread crumbs and Italian seasoning in another bowl. Roll the oiled cheese in bread crumbs, place on a small baking sheet and refrigerate 1 hour.

GREENS

❧Rinse greens, pat dry and slice into thin strips.

VINAIGRETTE

❧In a small bowl, whisk together all the vinaigrette ingredients until smooth.

❧To assemble, preheat oven to 400°F.

❧Bake breaded cheese until it is light brown, warm throughout and beginning to soften, approximately 8 to 10 minutes. Be careful not to overcook or cheese will melt and collapse.

❧Toss the vinaigrette with greens, transfer the greens to 8 salad plates and top with the hot cheese.

Serves 8.

During late spring, we enjoy this tasty and beautiful dish of fresh spinach and watercress from our garden combined with soft, warm California chevre (goat cheese) or Italian Gorgonzola.

POMODORI CLASSICI

Garden Tomatoes with Minced Herbs

I'm sure most gardeners and cooks have prepared vine-ripened tomatoes in a similar manner—but I couldn't resist including my favorite version. There is no combination of flavors quite so divine as sweet and juicy tomatoes just plucked from the vine, adorned with equally fresh snipped herbs.

If you choose to use peeled tomatoes, simply run the blade of a table or butter knife over the surface of the tomato, perpendicular to the skin, scraping it without puncturing it. Cut out the core and the skin easily pulls off.

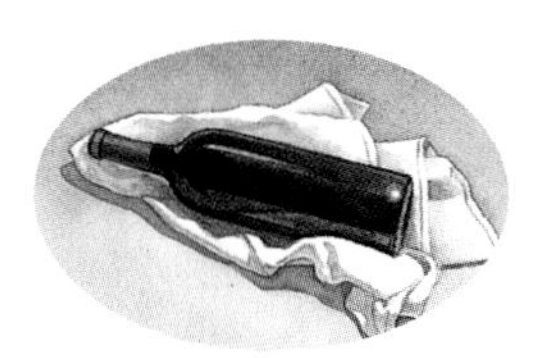

VIANSA WINE SUGGESTION
'Augusto' Barbera

4 large vine-ripened tomatoes, cored and sliced

3 tablespoons red wine

1 tablespoon freshly squeezed lemon juice

5 tablespoons Viansa Extra Virgin Olive Oil

1 tablespoon minced Italian parsley

2 tablespoons fresh basil chiffonade (basil leaves sliced into skinny little ribbons)

2 tablespoons minced fresh tarragon

1 tablespoon minced fresh chives

¼ teaspoon salt

Freshly ground black pepper to taste

Arrange tomato slices in a shallow serving dish. Whisk together wine, lemon juice and olive oil. Add fresh herbs, salt and pepper and mix well. Pour over the tomato slices and allow to stand at room temperature for an hour or so before serving. Accompany with crusty bread and a wedge of Pecorino cheese.

Serves 6 (about 3 slices each).

SPINACI ALL'AGRO

Baby Spinach with Lemon-Garlic Oil

3 tablespoons Viansa Extra Virgin Olive Oil

3 tablespoons freshly squeezed lemon juice

1 small clove garlic, minced

Pinch of kosher salt

Pinch of freshly ground black pepper

2½ pounds fresh baby spinach

❧Whisk together the olive oil, lemon juice, garlic, salt and pepper vigorously until dressing thickens.

❧Trim any tough stems from spinach leaves and rinse well by immersing in lots of cold water.

❧ If serving as a salad, spin leaves in a lettuce spinner or pat dry with paper towels. Toss with lemon-garlic oil. If serving hot with an entree, put rinsed spinach leaves (along with the water that clings to them from rinsing) into a very large saucepan. Cover and cook over low heat just until spinach has wilted. Drain, return to saucepan and toss with lemon garlic oil. Transfer to a hot serving platter.

Serves 4.

This recipe is a perfect example of the Tuscan fondness for pure, simple and natural flavors. If you have access to edible wild greens, by all means, use them! Otherwise, experiment with what is available at your market or use delicious fresh baby spinach greens. The greens can be served cold as a salad or hot to accompany an entree.

Cloudiness in olive oil does not indicate anything is wrong with the oil. On the contrary—if not caused by refrigeration, the sediment is a result of small bits of olive in the oil and adds flavor and color. The less processing and filtering, the thicker and more flavorful the oil!

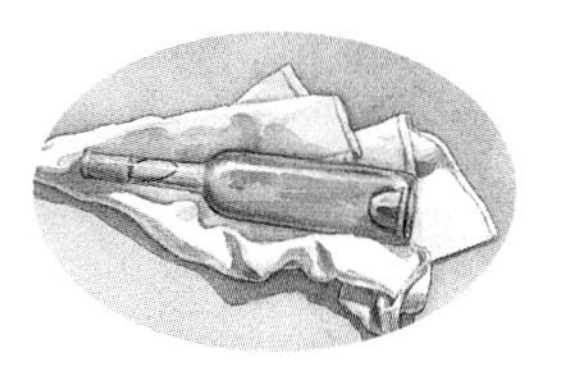

VIANSA WINE SUGGESTION
Sauvignon Blanc or Nebbiolo

Fresh Berries and Grapes with Sweet Balsamic Marinade

MACEDONI DI FRUTTA ALL'ACETO BALSAMICO

Fresh Berries and Grapes with Sweet Balsamic Marinade

1 pound green or red seedless grapes

2 baskets (12 ounces each) strawberries

1 basket (6 to 8 ounces) raspberries

1 basket (6 to 8 ounces) blueberries

1 basket (6 to 8 ounces) blackberries

BALSAMIC MARINADE

½ cup sugar

¼ cup Viansa 'Musecco' Muscat Canelli or 'Imbianco' Barbera Rosé

¼ cup Viansa Balsamic Vinegar

Trim and rinse all the fruit. Slice the strawberries in half and combine with the grapes and other berries in a large bowl.

BALSAMIC MARINADE

Whisk together the sugar, wine and vinegar until the sugar dissolves. Very gently toss the wine mixture with the fruit. Allow fruit to sit for 1 hour, gently tossing occasionally to allow the flavors to permeate the fruit.

Makes 12 cups.

Summer or winter, Viansa visitors love this combination of fresh berries and grapes mixed with fruity wine and dark, sweet balsamic vinegar. Many of our visitors enjoy this dish eaten as a salad, while others save it for dessert. Either way, this symphony of flavors is irresistible!

If you are unable to locate one of the berries suggested, substitute what is available in your market. Keep in mind that if you use light-colored fruit, the balsamic vinegar will turn it dark.

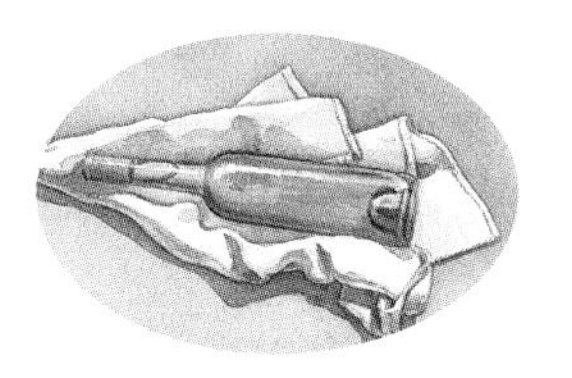

VIANSA WINE SUGGESTION

'Musecco' Muscat Canelli or 'Imbianco' Barbera Rosé

Zuppa e Pane

Soup, Calzone and Bread

Bread is one of the age-old staples of Tuscan cuisine,

and we honor our heritage by enjoying bread with every meal—

whether it is a hearty country loaf or Viansa's herb-laden focaccia.

A slice of homemade bread matched with a hearty bowl of soup

is a simple but satisfying meal that has no equal.

Villagers harvest grain in the countryside with Pisa in the distance.

ZUPPA DI SPINACI E BASILICO

Spinach and Basil Soup

The terms 'chicken stock' and 'chicken broth' have come to mean the same thing in most kitchens and are virtually interchangeable. They do share common ingredients (onion, carrots, celery and herbs), but chicken meat is traditionally used to flavor broth and chicken bones are used for stock. Either way, homemade chicken broth is far superior to canned and is also very quick, inexpensive and easy to prepare. I have included my version.

2 packages (10 ounces each) frozen chopped spinach

3 cups chicken broth (preferably homemade)

3 tablespoons olive oil

1 medium white or yellow onion, chopped

6 cloves garlic, minced

¼ cup fresh basil leaves

1 teaspoon salt

¼ teaspoon white pepper

Place frozen spinach in a large saucepan with chicken broth. Cover and cook for 6 to 8 minutes, until spinach is just cooked.

Heat oil in a medium-sized skillet and sauté onion and garlic for 2 to 3 minutes. Stir in basil leaves and cook 1 more minute.

Pour the cooked spinach and broth into a blender or food processor and add onion mixture, salt and pepper. Purée until creamy. Return to the saucepan and gently heat. Be careful not to overcook the soup or it will turn brown.

Serves 4.

HOMEMADE CHICKEN STOCK OR BROTH: I purchase a 5-pound bag of chicken backs from the market, trim off all fat and combine 2 of the chicken backs (I keep the rest on hand in the freezer) with 3 quarts of water. If I have time, I add one or more of the following: large chunks of onion, carrot, celery, whole garlic cloves and greens such as celery tops, parsley, thyme, bay leaf or other herbs, salt and a few peppercorns. Bring to a boil (skim foam if necessary) and simmer for about 45 minutes. Remove the vegetables and you have homemade chicken broth! If I am in a hurry, I omit the vegetables and just cook the chicken in water, which still makes a very flavorful broth. Store extra broth in the refrigerator for 5 or 6 days, or freeze.

GAZPACHO ALLA CALIFORNIA

Chilled California Garden Gazpacho

1 large cucumber, peeled, seeded and diced

1 large red onion, peeled and diced

1 large red bell pepper, cored, seeded and diced

1 large zucchini, diced

6 large tomatoes, peeled, seeded and diced (about 6 cups)

¼ cup white wine

2 cups tomato juice

3 tablespoons Viansa Extra Virgin Olive Oil

1 tablespoon freshly squeezed lemon juice

1 tablespoon Viansa Balsamic Vinegar

1 large clove garlic, minced

1 teaspoon salt

¼ teaspoon pepper

Dash Tabasco sauce

GARNISH

½ cup sour cream

½ cup minced fresh chives

½ cup croutons, preferably homemade

Set aside ½ cup each of the chopped cucumber, red onion, red pepper and zucchini. In a blender or food processor combine the rest of the vegetables with the remaining ingredients. Purée slightly, so vegetables are left a little chunky. Combine soup with the reserved vegetables, cover tightly with plastic wrap and chill 2 to 3 hours. To serve, top with a dollop of sour cream, a sprinkle of minced chives and several croutons.

Makes 8 cups.

All year long I dream about our garden tomatoes finally becoming ripe enough so that I can make this refreshing cold soup. Gazpacho is a cold Mexican soup that has become a favorite of Californians. Though there is no Italian translation, Tuscans combine the same flavorful ingredients during summer months.

In addition to being refreshing, tasty and nutritious, it has the additional advantage of being low in fat and calories.

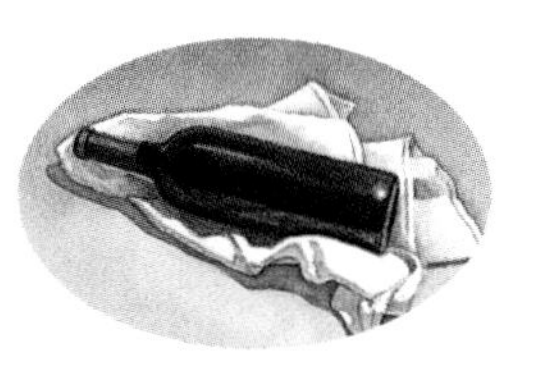

VIANSA WINE SUGGESTION

'Augusto' Barbera or Nebbiolo

Tuscan Bean and Sausage Soup, Tuscan Country Bread

MINESTRA ALLA TOSCANA

Tuscan Bean and Sausage Soup

1½ cups dried white beans

4 cups chicken broth (preferably homemade)

1 can (6 ounces) tomato paste

2 tablespoons minced garlic

1 tablespoon minced fresh rosemary

2 teaspoons dried oregano

2 teaspoons dried thyme

2 cups chopped celery

2 cups chopped leeks, white parts only

1 large yellow onion, chopped

1½ pounds Italian sausage (about 3 sausages), cut into pieces

2 tablespoons olive oil

2 large tomatoes, seeded and chopped

4 tablespoons minced fresh basil

1 teaspoon salt

½ teaspoon freshly ground black pepper

Rinse the beans well, place in a large pot and cover with water. Bring to a boil, reduce heat and simmer 45 minutes. Drain beans and return to the pot. Add the chicken broth, tomato paste, garlic, rosemary, oregano and thyme. Cook 30 minutes over medium-high heat.

Sauté the chopped celery, leeks, onion and sausage in the olive oil for 20 minutes. Add to the beans along with the chopped tomatoes, basil, salt and pepper, and cook over medium-low heat until hot.

Serves 6 (about 2 cups each).

A staple during cold winter months at Viansa and Lo Spuntino, this soup is anxiously awaited by regular visitors. It seems like the more miserable the weather gets, the better the soup tastes! Accompanied by a slice of fresh or toasted Tuscan Country Bread (recipe on page 110) and a glass of robust red wine, this soup is guaranteed to warm the heart and soul.

Minestra, which implies a thicker, heartier soup, is another Italian dish that is prepared differently in each region—and most certainly by each chef. "Alla Toscana" means "Tuscan style" and it includes dried white beans, rosemary and chopped ham. This is my version of Minestra Alla Toscana.

VIANSA WINE SUGGESTION

'Riserva Anatra Rosso' Cabernet Sauvignon,
Cabernet Sauvignon or
'Piccolo Toscano' Sangiovese

PANE RUSTICO

Tuscan Country Bread

As this recipe shows, making bread is really a rather simple procedure. Just be sure to check the expiration date on the package of yeast you use to make sure it isn't too old to rise.

Tailor this hearty loaf to your own tastes by adding your favorite chopped herbs, diced cheese, seeds, nuts, or even cooked vegetables.

VIANSA WINE SUGGESTION
'Piccolo Toscano' Sangiovese or 'Riserva Anatra Bianco' Trebbiano

1 package (¼ ounce) active dry yeast

1½ cups lukewarm water

½ cup white wine, slightly warmed

2¼ cups unbleached white flour

2 cups whole wheat flour

½ teaspoon sugar

¼ teaspoon salt

⅓ cup oil-packed sun-dried tomatoes, drained and cut into strips

⅓ cup kalamata olives, pitted and quartered

To Mix Using an Electric Mixer: In a small bowl, stir the yeast into the water and wine to dissolve. Set aside for about 3 to 5 minutes. Combine both flours, sugar and salt into the large bowl of the mixer and mix together (using a dough hook if you have one). Stir the yeast mixture again and then slowly pour it into the flour mixture, with the mixer running on low speed. Increase the speed to medium and continue mixing until the dough forms a solid, soft mass. Add the sun-dried tomatoes and the olives and continue mixing until the dough is soft and elastic.

To Mix Using a Food Processor: In a small bowl, stir the yeast into the water and wine to dissolve. Set aside for about 3 to 5 minutes. Combine both flours, sugar and salt in food processor bowl and pulse slightly to mix. Stir the yeast mixture again and then drizzle it into the flour mixture with the processor running. Process on full power until the dough spins in one solid, soft mass. Add sun-dried tomatoes and olives and process until the dough is soft and elastic.

Grease a small baking sheet. Shape the dough into a round or oval loaf and place on the baking sheet. Dust the top of the dough very lightly with flour, cover with a kitchen towel and let the dough rise in a warm place for 1 hour (a good place is in a cold oven with only the oven light turned on to warm it).

About 15 minutes before the hour is up, preheat your oven to 425°F (if the dough is rising in your oven, be sure to take it out first!). Bake the dough on a greased baking sheet for 10 minutes. Reduce heat to 400°F and continue baking for 20 to 25 minutes longer, or until golden brown.

Makes 1 loaf, about 2½ pounds.

(See photograph on page 108.)

CALZONE SPUNTINO

Lo Spuntino Calzone

CRUST

1½ cups warm water

2 teaspoons honey

2 packages (¼ ounce each) active dry yeast

3½ cups all-purpose flour

½ cup bread flour

¾ teaspoon salt

1 teaspoon olive oil

FILLING

1 medium portobello mushroom (about 4 ounces), cut into ¼-inch thick slices

10 to 12 mushrooms (about 3 to 4 ounces), such as cremini, shiitake or button

2 to 3 tablespoons olive oil

4 chicken sausages or Italian sausages (about 1 pound)

1 small bulb fennel, chopped

1 small red onion, chopped

1 red bell pepper, cut into matchstick-sized pieces

1 yellow bell pepper, cut into matchstick-sized pieces

3 tablespoons each thyme leaves and minced Italian parsley

½ cup roasted garlic (about 32 cloves)

4 ounces fontina cheese, cubed

1 tablespoon olive oil

CRUST

In a small bowl, mix together the warm water, honey and yeast. Set aside for 20 minutes, or until bubbles form on the surface.

Place both flours and the salt in a food processor or electric mixer. With motor running, drizzle yeast mixture into the flours. Process or mix for 2 minutes, adding more water if necessary (a teaspoon at a time) until dough forms a ball.

Spread the teaspoon of olive oil over the surface of a large glass or stainless steel bowl and transfer the dough ball to it. Cover with a clean kitchen towel and allow to rise in a warm place for 1 hour.

FILLING

Lightly brush the mushrooms to clean. Sauté with olive oil in a large skillet until hot throughout. Remove and transfer to a large bowl. In the same pan, sauté the whole sausages until barely cooked. Cut into bite-size pieces and transfer to the bowl with the mushrooms. Add the chopped fennel, onion, red and yellow peppers, thyme, parsley, roasted garlic and fontina cheese. Toss to combine.

Preheat the oven to 375°F. On parchment paper or a floured surface, roll out the dough to a 14 by 14-inch square. Work carefully, as the dough is fairly soft. Fold the dough slightly and transfer to a parchment-lined (or greased) baking sheet. Unfold the dough and mound the filling mixture across the bottom of the square. Fold the dough over the mound to form a log. Stuff any stray filling into the log and pinch along the side and ends to seal the dough. Brush the top with 1 tablespoon olive oil, and sprinkle with kosher salt, if desired. Cut 3 or 4 slashes across the top to allow steam to escape during cooking.

Bake for 50 minutes, until crust is golden brown.

Serves 10 to 12.

Although slightly cumbersome, this flavor packed pizza-like creation reminds me of a giant omelet. Whatever abundant or leftover vegetables you have on hand can be tucked into a crust, baked and presented to a small army of hungry mouths.

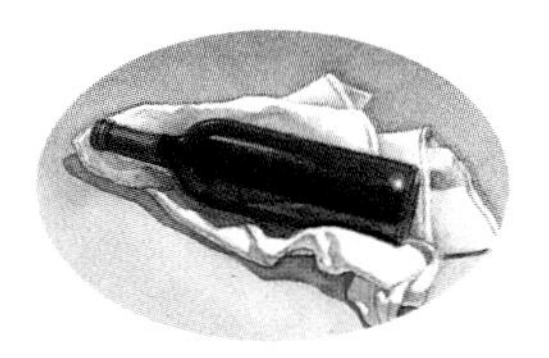

VIANSA WINE SUGGESTION

'Thalia' Sangiovese, 'Piccolo Toscano' Sangiovese or 'Riserva Anatra Bianco' Trebbiano

Viansa's Foccacia Bread

FOCCACIA VIANSA

Viansa's Foccacia Bread

1 package (¼ ounce) active dry yeast

1 cup lukewarm water

2½ cups bread flour

1 teaspoon dried oregano

1 teaspoon dried thyme

1 teaspoon minced fresh rosemary

2 tablespoons Viansa Extra Virgin Olive Oil

2 teaspoons kosher salt

In a small bowl, stir the yeast into the water to dissolve. Set aside for 3 to 5 minutes.

TO MIX USING AN ELECTRIC MIXER: Combine the flour and herbs in the large mixing bowl and mix together (using a dough hook if you have one). Stir the yeast mixture again and slowly pour it into the flour mixture with the mixer running on low speed. Turn the speed up and continue mixing about 3 minutes, until the dough forms a solid, soft mass. Drizzle 1 tablespoon of the olive oil into the dough and continue mixing until the dough is elastic. Remove the dough to a floured surface and knead to make a ball.

TO MIX USING A FOOD PROCESSOR: Combine the flour and herbs in the food processor bowl and pulse slightly to mix. Stir the yeast mixture again and then drizzle it into the flour mixture with the processor running. Process on full power only until the dough spins in one solid, soft mass. Drizzle 1 tablespoon oil into the dough and continue mixing for about 1 minute, until the dough is elastic. Remove the dough to a floured surface and knead to make a ball.

Spread the remaining tablespoon of olive oil over the surface of a large glass or stainless steel bowl and transfer the dough ball to it. Cover the bowl with a kitchen towel and let the dough rise in a warm place for 45 minutes (a good place is in a cold oven with only the oven light turned on to warm it).

Punch down the dough (poking dough with your fingers) and stretch it to form a rectangle on a floured surface. Let it rest five minutes. Roll out the dough and fit it onto an oiled 16x18-inch baking pan or sheet.

Cover with a kitchen towel and let the dough rest for 45 minutes. After 30 minutes, preheat the oven to 400°F. Remove the towel, poke 8 to 10 holes in the dough with a fork, brush with remaining tablespoon olive oil and sprinkle with salt.

Bake 30 minutes. Halfway through baking, rotate the bread in the oven. Remove when golden brown on top. Transfer bread to a wire rack to cool.

Makes 1 loaf.

We use kosher salt exclusively in our kitchens. We prefer its flaky texture and natural flavor to that of refined salt. The sprinkling of kosher salt on the top of the prepared dough is what gives our signature Viansa Foccacia its character.

Due to its lighter consistency, kosher salt cannot be substituted for equal amounts of table salt. So if you have to use table salt in a recipe, use half the amount of required kosher salt. However, it's worth it to try to find kosher salt, as the difference is remarkable.

Many, many visitors have enjoyed Viansa's Foccacia Bread dunked or dipped into Viansa Extra Virgin Olive Oil. For a special treat, serve it with my Dipping Oil recipe on page 17.

VIANSA WINE SUGGESTION

Any wine you like!

PANE DI GRANTURCO DOPPIO CON PEPE

Jalapeño Double-Corn Bread

For a crisper crust, wipe a little olive oil into the muffin tins or baking pan and heat for 5 minutes or so in a hot oven before adding the batter.

1 package (8½ ounces) corn muffin mix

1¼ cups milk

1 small white onion, minced

1 cup canned cream-style corn

2 teaspoons sugar

1 can (4 ounces) diced green chiles

2 eggs, well beaten

1 cup coarsely shredded sharp cheddar cheese (about 4 ounces)

Preheat oven to 400°F.

Combine all the ingredients in a large mixing bowl and beat to mix thoroughly. Bake in greased muffin tins or in a 9x13-inch baking pan for 40 to 45 minutes. Allow corn bread to cool for 15 to 20 minutes, and then cut into 3-inch squares.

Makes 12 muffins or squares.

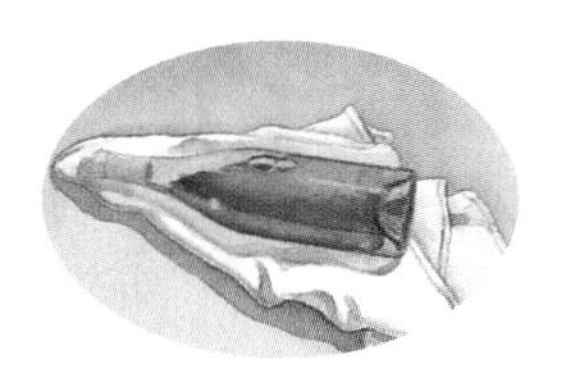

VIANSA WINE SUGGESTION
'Riserva Anatra Bianco' Trebbiano

CIALDE DI FORMAGGIO ALLE ERBE

Herbed Cheese Wafers

2 cups all-purpose flour

⅔ cup cold unsalted butter (5½ ounces)

1¾ cups shredded sharp cheddar cheese (about 4 ounces)

Pinch of crushed red pepper

3 tablespoons dry white wine

2 teaspoons crushed dried basil

2 teaspoons crushed dried oregano

2 teaspoons freshly grated Parmesan cheese

Preheat oven to 350°F.

Place flour in large bowl or in work bowl of food processor. Cut in butter until mixture resembles coarse meal. Stir in cheddar cheese and crushed red pepper. Sprinkle with wine and gently combine without overworking the dough; work just until it forms a solid ball.

Roll out the dough to ¼-inch thickness on lightly floured surface. Cut into squares using a fluted pastry wheel, into circles with a canapé cutter, or into the shape of your choice. Combine herbs and Parmesan cheese and sprinkle over the wafers. Transfer to a lightly-buttered baking sheet (wafers can be placed close together as they do not spread). Bake until lightly brown, about 12 to 15 minutes. Transfer to wire rack to cool. Wafers can be stored in a sealed tin for several weeks.

VARIATION: To make Herbed Cheese Sticks, combine the herbs with the dough and cut dough into 3-inch by ¼-inch strips.

Makes about 6 to 8 dozen wafers, depending on size.

When my annual herbs are nearing the end of their growth cycle, I often microwave them for a few minutes between paper towels to dry them for future use. Stored in an airtight container in a cool dark place, they will last for up to 6 months.

If you are cooking with dried herbs and they seem to lack flavor, simply add a little more than the recipe calls for.

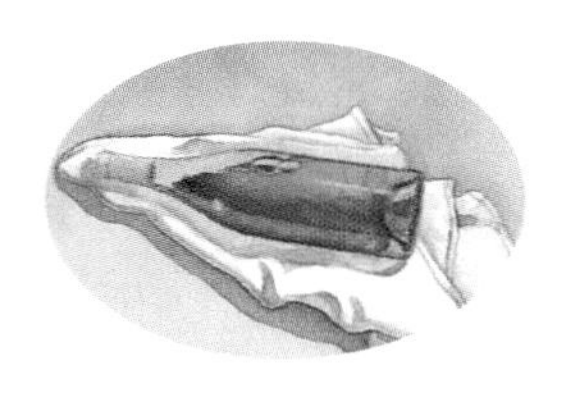

VIANSA WINE SUGGESTION
Chardonnay or 'Piccolo Toscano' Sangiovese

Dolci

Desserts

No meal at Viansa is complete without dessert,

and our favorites run the gamut from simple to spectacular.

Some nights we indulge in a rich and decadent Tuscan tiramisù,

on others we may delight in the simple joys of

perfectly-baked biscotti dipped in wine.

Blood oranges, a favorite Tuscan sweet, are harvested in the orchards outside Farneta.

SOUFFLÉ DI CIOCCOLATO E ARACHIDI

Chocolate Peanut Soufflé

Many cooks, even experienced ones, are afraid of soufflés. This fear is largely unfounded as you'll realize when you try my simple recipe.

The worst thing that can happen is that your soufflé will fall. Not to worry. You can call it a pudding and it will still taste divine!

VIANSA WINE SUGGESTION
Reserve Cabernet Sauvignon, 'Athena' Dolcetto or 'Musecco' Muscat Canelli

1 tablespoon butter

3 tablespoons finely chopped unsalted peanuts

½ cup chunky-style peanut butter

8 egg whites, at room temperature

½ cup sugar

2 tablespoons Viansa Raspberry di Cioccolato Sauce, slightly melted (or another thick, rich chocolate sauce)

Generously butter a 1½-quart soufflé dish. Sprinkle the bottom and sides with chopped peanuts.

Preheat oven to 450°F.

Place the peanut butter in a medium-size bowl and set aside. In the large bowl of an electric mixer, beat the egg whites on medium-high speed until frothy. Gradually drizzle in the sugar and beat on high speed until soft peaks form.

Stir about 1 cup of the beaten egg whites into the peanut butter, stirring until the mixture is smooth and even colored. Gently fold the peanut butter mixture into the remaining beaten egg whites (be careful not to overmix). Gently spoon into the prepared soufflé dish.

Drizzle the melted chocolate over soufflé mixture. Gently swirl a knife through the soufflé to create a chocolate ribbon effect. Be careful not to scrape peanuts from the sides of the dish.

Place soufflé dish in center of preheated oven and immediately reduce temperature to 375°F. Bake for 20 to 25 minutes, until a knife inserted near the center of the soufflé comes out clean. Do not overbake. Serve the soufflé immediately, as it will collapse rather quickly.

Serves 6 to 8.

PESCHE CON NOCI E CIOCCOLATO

Pecan-Coated Peaches with Chocolate Sauce

⅓ cup Viansa 'Musecco' Muscat Canelli

4 large peaches

4 tablespoons butter, melted

4 tablespoons brown sugar

½ cup pecans, toasted and finely chopped

⅓ cup Viansa Raspberry Di Cioccolato Sauce (or another thick, rich chocolate sauce)

❧Preheat oven to 350°F.

❧Rinse peaches and cut in half, removing the pits. Slice off the rounded ends so the peach halves will sit flat. Pour wine into a shallow baking dish and soak the peach halves in the wine for 5 minutes. Turn over and soak the second side for 5 minutes. Combine melted butter and brown sugar in a small bowl. Dip each peach half in the butter-sugar mixture, turning to coat each side. Put chopped nuts in a small bowl and pat each side of buttered peach half into the chopped nuts to coat.

❧Place nut-coated peach halves, cut side up, on a large baking sheet and bake for 15 minutes.

❧Carefully heat the chocolate sauce until melted and hot. Place baked peach halves on a serving platter, or serve individually. Drizzle about 2 teaspoons hot chocolate sauce over each peach half and serve hot.

Serves 8.

If you prefer peeled peaches and your peaches are firm enough, use a vegetable peeler to remove the skin. If they are not, either soak the peaches in boiling water for a few minutes (off the stove) or microwave them for 10 seconds and let them sit for another 5 seconds. They should then peel easily.

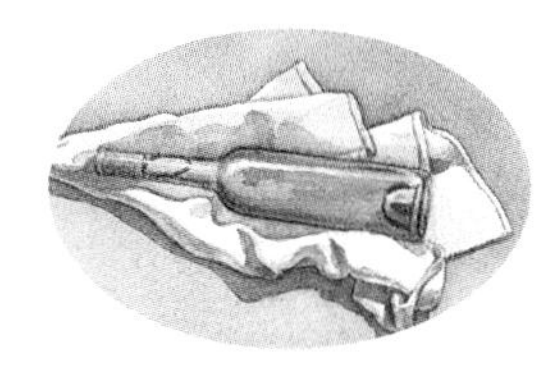

VIANSA WINE SUGGESTION

'Musecco' Muscat Canelli or 'Imbianco' Barbera Rosé

Chocolate Cheesecake Tart

CROSTATA DI CIOCCOLATO

Chocolate Cheesecake Tart

CRUST
1 cup all-purpose flour

⅓ cup powdered sugar

2 rounded tablespoons cocoa powder

1 rounded teaspoon instant coffee (not freeze-dried)

½ cup + 2 tablespoons cold unsalted butter (1¼ sticks), cut into small pieces

FILLING
12 ounces cream cheese, at room temperature

1 rounded tablespoon cocoa powder

1 rounded teaspoon instant coffee (not freeze-dried)

½ cup powdered sugar

1 large egg

½ teaspoon vanilla

TOPPING
1 basket (6 ounces) raspberries

3 peaches or nectarines, pitted and thinly sliced

4 strawberries, cut in half

12 blackberries

GLAZE
⅔ cup apricot jam

CRUST

Preheat oven to 350°F.

Combine flour, sugar, cocoa powder, coffee and butter in a food processor and process until dough forms a large ball (or mix dough using your usual pie crust method). Press dough to about ⅛-inch thickness on the bottom and up the sides of a 9-inch fluted tart, quiche or pie pan with sides ¾ to 1-inch high. Bake the crust for 10 minutes. Remove from oven and set aside.

FILLING

Reduce oven temperature to 325°F. In a food processor or mixer, mix the filling ingredients until smooth. Spoon the filling into the baked crust and bake for 30 minutes. Remove from the oven and allow to cool at least 15 minutes before adding the fruit topping.

TOPPING

Arrange the fruit decoratively over the cooled filling.

GLAZE

In a small saucepan, heat the apricot jam over very low heat until hot, about 3 minutes. Stir continuously, as it burns easily. When the jam is hot, press it through a strainer into a small bowl. Discard the chunks of apricot or save for another use. Keep the remaining syrupy part warm, carefully reheating if necessary. Brush or spoon over the fruit, coating well.

Serves 8 to 10.

According to some Italian officials, the ancient Romans invented cheesecakes. Their first attempts were pretty basic, dry and flavorless. Eventually their love of cheese led them to sweeter varieties, which also led to tastier cheesecakes.

When making this tart, feel free to use any fresh fruit that you wish! My kids love bananas on the top (just be sure to glaze immediately to prevent browning). I have even used canned fruit at times when I haven't had fresh fruit on hand, and have been just as happy with the results.

VIANSA WINE SUGGESTION
'Athena' Dolcetto, 'Imbianco' Barbera Rosé or 'Musecco' Muscat Canelli

CROSTATA DI NOCI ALL'ESPRESSO

Espresso Walnut Tart

I usually use unsalted butter when preparing tart or pie crusts. Salt is added to butter as a preservative, so unsalted butter is usually fresher than salted butter. A pinch of salt is then added for flavor.

VIANSA WINE SUGGESTION
'Athena' Dolcetto or 'Di Pacomio' Aleatico

CRUST

1 cup all-purpose flour

⅓ cup powdered sugar

½ cup cold unsalted butter (1 stick), cut into small pieces

Pinch of salt

FILLING

2 tablespoons instant espresso powder

2 tablespoons hot water

½ cup brown sugar, firmly packed

4 eggs

2 tablespoons rum

⅓ cup light corn syrup

¼ cup unsalted butter (½ stick), melted

Pinch of salt

2 cups finely chopped walnuts, toasted

CRUST

Preheat oven to 350°F.

Combine flour, sugar, butter and salt in a food processor and process until the dough forms a large ball (or mix dough using your usual pie crust method). Press dough to about ⅛-inch thickness on the bottom and up the sides of a 9-inch fluted tart, quiche or pie pan with sides ¾ to 1-inch high. Bake for 20 minutes, until light golden brown. Remove from oven and set aside.

FILLING

Preheat oven to 375°F.

In a large bowl, dissolve espresso powder in hot water. Whisk in brown sugar until smooth. Add eggs, rum, corn syrup, butter and salt. Whisk until well combined. Stir in walnuts. Place the pan with the crust on a baking sheet and pour the filling into it.

Carefully transfer the baking sheet with the filled tart to the oven and bake for 10 minutes at 375°F. Reduce the oven temperature to 350°F and continue baking for 35 to 45 minutes, until center is slightly raised, lightly browned and a wooden pick inserted in the center comes out clean.

Serves 8 to 10.

CROSTATA AL DON SILVIO

Don Silvio's Vegetable Dessert Tart

CRUST
1 cup all-purpose flour
¼ cup powdered sugar
½ cup cold unsalted butter (1 stick), cut into small pieces

FILLING
⅓ cup fruity white wine (such as Viansa 'Musecco' Muscat Canelli or 'Imbianco' Barbera Rosé)
⅔ cup golden raisins
2 cups coarsely chopped green chard leaves
2 cups grated zucchini (about 2 medium zucchini)
8 small leaves fresh basil, minced
8 small leaves fresh mint, minced
½ cup finely chopped walnuts
¼ cup honey
4 eggs, lightly beaten

CRUST

Combine flour, powdered sugar and butter in a food processor and process until the dough forms a large ball (or mix dough using your usual pie crust method). Press dough to about ⅛-inch thickness on the bottom and up the sides of a 9-inch fluted tart, quiche or pie pan with sides ¾ to 1-inch high (preferably a pan with a removable rim). Set aside.

FILLING

Preheat oven to 375°F.

Warm the wine and soak the raisins for 15 to 20 minutes. Drain raisins, saving the wine. Combine the wine with half the chard and zucchini in a blender or food processor. Purée slightly. Combine all the remaining ingredients in a large bowl. Add the puréed ingredients, mix thoroughly and pour into crust.

Bake 50 to 55 minutes, until filling has set and a wooden pick inserted in the center comes out clean. Cool in the pan 30 minutes before removing the rim or serving. Serve at room temperature.

Serves 8 to 10.

During our travels throughout Italy, we see vegetables used in many sweets, such as cakes, tarts and cookies. Green tomato tarts, sweet onion tarts, cookies with corn and polenta, small dense cakes with rice and basil — all are sweetened with either raisins, bits of dried fruit, honey or chocolate. One of the most popular, and most unusual, is this chard and zucchini tart.

Many years ago when we first visited the 12th century village of Farneta, where Sam's grandfather Samuele grew up, the local church priest, Don Silvio, served this unusual dessert for us. We liked it so much that I created this recipe when we returned home.

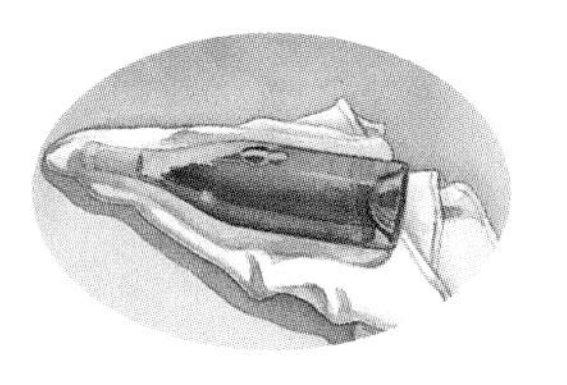

VIANSA WINE SUGGESTION

'Riserva Anatra Bianco' Trebbiano, 'Musecco' Muscat Canelli or 'Imbianco' Barbera Rosé

Chocolate Polenta Cheesecake

TORTA DI RICOTTA AL CIOCCOLATO

Chocolate Polenta Cheesecake

CRUST

24 Oreo cookies

¼ cup butter, melted

FILLING

2 cups ricotta cheese

½ cup granulated sugar

1 tablespoon + 1 teaspoon grated lemon zest

3 tablespoons freshly squeezed lemon juice

2 dashes ground cinnamon

4 large eggs

4½ cups milk

1 teaspoon salt

1½ cups polenta

⅓ cup Viansa Raspberry Di Cioccolato Sauce (or other rich, thick chocolate sauce)

CRUST

Process the cookies in a food processor until finely chopped (or crush in a plastic bag with a rolling pin). Add the melted butter and mix until completely incorporated. Press crust along the bottom and one inch up the sides of an 8 or 9-inch springform pan. Set aside.

FILLING

Preheat oven to 375°F.

In the large bowl of a food processor or a mixer, combine the ricotta cheese, sugar, lemon zest, lemon juice and cinnamon, mixing well. Add eggs one at a time, pulsing briefly (or mixing on medium speed) after addition of each egg, to combine well.

In a large heavy saucepan, heat milk over medium-high heat just to boiling point, then add salt. Lower heat and slowly drizzle polenta into hot milk, stirring continuously to prevent lumping. Cook on medium-low heat for approximately 5 minutes, until polenta is thick and smooth, stirring frequently to prevent scorching on the bottom of the pan. When cooked, allow to cool slightly. Add by large spoonfuls to the cheese and egg mixture, pulsing (or mixing on medium speed) after each addition to blend into mixture. When thoroughly blended, pour into crust.

Warm chocolate sauce to a thick syrup-like consistency in microwave or double boiler. Drizzle and stir slightly into cheesecake, being very careful not to touch the crust on sides or bottom.

Bake 1 hour and 10 minutes. Place a cookie sheet or aluminum foil underneath while baking, as the crust will leak and dribble somewhat in the oven. Remove from the oven and allow cheesecake to sit for at least an hour before serving. You can refrigerate the cheesecake, but it is not necessary. Just before serving, place 1 or 2 espresso beans on each slice, if desired.

Serves 12.

Corn is native to the Western Hemisphere and was introduced to Italian cuisine from America in the 16th century. Polenta, Italians' favorite corn product, is available in fine, medium and coarse grinds.

Preferences for grind, as well as cooking time, are once again a source for regional argument. All cooks, Italian and American, do agree, however, to slowly drizzle the cornmeal into the pot and continuously stir to prevent lumping and exploding grains.

VIANSA WINE SUGGESTION
'Athena' Dolcetto

TORTA DI FORMAGGIO CON BISCOTTI E LIMONE

Lemon Biscotti Cheesecake

If you would like to make the recipe using another type of cookie for the crust, just substitute a hard, dry cookie. If in doubt about the hardness of the cookies, simply bake the crushed cookies a little longer, until they are crunchy.

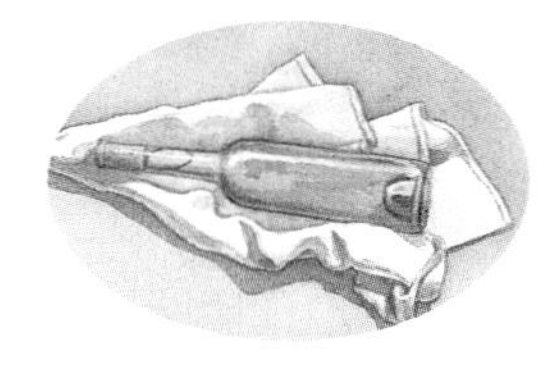

VIANSA WINE SUGGESTION
'Musecco' Muscat Canelli or 'Imbianco' Barbera Rosé

CRUST

8 biscotti, approximately 6 ounces each

3 tablespoons butter, melted

FILLING

1 cup mascarpone cheese (or cream cheese)

1 cup ricotta cheese

¾ cup sugar

2 teaspoons minced lemon zest

3 tablespoons freshly squeezed lemon juice

3 eggs

LEMON CURD TOPPING

1 teaspoon cornstarch

⅓ cup freshly squeezed lemon juice

5 egg yolks, beaten well

½ cup sugar

1 tablespoon butter, softened and cut into small pieces

CRUST

Preheat oven to 325°F.

Using a food processor (or a rolling pin) crush the biscotti until finely chopped. Spread the crumbs on a cookie sheet and bake for about 5 minutes. Transfer to a medium-size bowl and combine with the melted butter. Pat the crust on the bottom and about 1 inch up the sides of an 8 to 9-inch springform pan.

FILLING

Combine all filling ingredients in a mixer or food processor and mix until smooth and creamy. Pour into crust and bake 1 hour. Cool at least 30 minutes before adding the topping.

LEMON CURD TOPPING

In a small bowl, combine the cornstarch with about 1 tablespoon lemon juice, making a paste. Stir in remaining lemon juice. Add beaten egg yolks and sugar and whisk until combined. Transfer to a double boiler and cook until warm. (If you don't wish to use a double boiler, pour lemon mixture into a small nonstick skillet over very low heat. Whisk continually to prevent egg yolks from setting and scorching. Cook until warm.) Stir in the butter and continue stirring. Cook until very thick, but still a pouring consistency.

Pour warm topping over cooled cheesecake. Refrigerate cheesecake for at least 1 hour. Run a knife between crust and removable rim to loosen. Remove the rim and serve.

Serves 12.

TORTA DI VINO E NOCI

Pecan Wine Cake

2 cups sugar

2½ cups light brown sugar (one 1-pound box)

1½ cups butter (3 sticks), at room temperature

6 eggs

5½ cups all-purpose flour

¼ teaspoon salt

1 teaspoon mace

2 cups fruity white wine (such as Viansa 'Musecco' Muscat Canelli or 'Imbianco' Barbera Rosé)

3 cups pecans, coarsely chopped

Preheat oven to 300°F.

Butter a 10-inch tube pan.

Mix the two sugars together and set aside. Cream the butter with an electric mixer until soft and fluffy. Add half of the sugar mixture (small amounts at a time) to the creamed butter. Increase the mixer speed and beat until smooth. In a large bowl, beat the eggs with a whisk until light and fluffy. Gradually whisk the remaining sugar mixture into the eggs. Continue whisking until you have a smooth, creamy consistency. Combine this mixture thoroughly with the butter mixture.

Stir together the flour, salt and mace. Alternately add the flour mixture and wine to the butter and egg mixture, mixing well after each addition. Stir the pecans into the batter.

Pour the batter into the prepared pan and bake for approximately 2 to 2¼ hours, until the cake is golden brown and a knife comes out clean when inserted. Cool for 30 minutes, then turn out onto a cake rack to cool completely.

This cake is very moist and it benefits from a day's aging prior to serving. To age, wrap in foil or plastic wrap and refrigerate. However, do not freeze.

Since Pecan Wine Cake is very rich, a small slice is sufficient. This cake should provide 24 generous pieces, and it will keep in the refrigerator for a week.

NOTE: I use a 10-inch tube pan (a large flat-bottomed cake pan with high sides and a removable bottom plate that is shaped into a tube in the center). If you don't have one, use a Bundt pan instead—you just won't be able to use all the batter. You can fill it to the rim, however, as the cake will only rise in the center of the batter-filled area and shouldn't overflow. Bake any excess cake batter in muffin tins for 1 to 1½ hours, or until a knife comes out clean when inserted.

Serves 24.

I often use this recipe for a buffet when I need a dessert that is not terribly sweet. It is a large cake, and small slices go a long way. It is also suitable for a morning coffee or ladies' party. It has the added bonus of staying tasty after a week in the refrigerator.

VIANSA WINE SUGGESTION

'Di Pacomio' Aleatico, 'Athena' Dolcetto, 'Musecco' Muscat Canelli or 'Imbianco' Barbera Rosé

Party Biscotti with Dried Fruit

BISCOTTI DI FESTA TUTTI FRUTTI

Party Biscotti with Dried Fruit

¼ cup butter (½ stick), at room temperature

1 cup sugar

1 teaspoon baking powder

½ teaspoon baking soda

¼ teaspoon salt

4 eggs

½ teaspoon vanilla extract

¼ teaspoon almond extract

2¼ cups flour

1½ teaspoons anise seed

½ teaspoon fennel seed

1 cup dried, sweetened cranberries

¾ cup shelled pistachios

½ cup diced dried apricots

In an electric mixer, beat the butter for about 30 seconds. Add the sugar, baking powder, baking soda and salt and beat until combined. Beat in 3 of the eggs, the vanilla and almond extracts. Beat in as much of the flour as you can with the mixer, until it becomes too stiff to mix. Stir in the remaining flour, the anise and fennel seeds, cranberries, pistachios and apricots by hand. Transfer dough to a lightly-floured surface. Roll into a ball, cover and refrigerate for several hours or until firm enough to handle easily.

Preheat oven to 350°F.

Divide the dough into two equal portions. Shape each portion into a log 12-inches long and 1½-inches in diameter. Place the logs at least 3 inches apart on a greased baking sheet. Pat down each log to ¾-inch thickness. Beat the fourth egg with 1 tablespoon water to make an egg wash. Brush logs with egg wash. Bake for 25 to 30 minutes or until light golden brown. Remove from oven and cool 1 hour.

Reduce oven temperature to 325°F.

Transfer biscotti logs to a cutting board and cut into ½-inch thick diagonal slices. Place the slices, cut side down, on baking sheet and bake 5 minutes. Turn biscotti over and bake another 5 minutes.

Makes approximately 48 biscotti.

Biscotti are extremely popular Italian-style cookies that are seen in virtually every restaurant and every home. While growing in availability in the United States, they command high prices in specialty food stores. Once you discover how easy and fun they are to make, you'll never buy them again. Biscotti are delicious dunked in red wine, coffee or grappa.

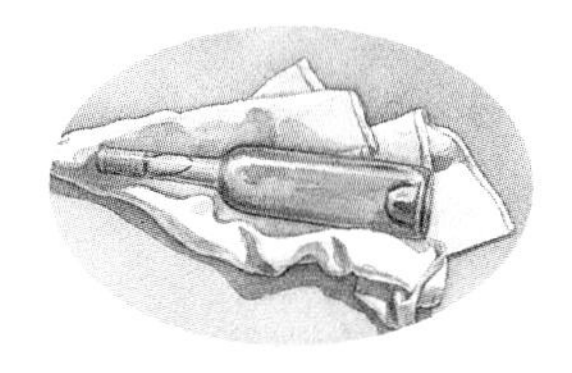

VIANSA WINE SUGGESTION

'Regalo di Certosa' Grappa, 'Ossidiana' Cabernet Franc/ Cabernet Sauvignon, or Prindelo

CIALDE AL LIMONE

Lemon Wafers

Biscotti, foccacina, cialda, pasticcino — whichever name you choose, Italians love cookies. They are usually dry and hard, and often have dollops of jam or chocolate on top. Many are designed for special holidays, feasts or celebrations. This cookie resembles one Venetians make to celebrate St. Martin's Day.

½ cup unsalted butter (1 stick), at room temperature

1 tablespoon finely grated lemon zest

¼ teaspoon almond extract

1 cup flour

½ cup powdered sugar

1 tablespoon cornstarch

¼ teaspoon salt

ICING

⅔ cup sifted powdered sugar

2 to 2½ teaspoons freshly squeezed lemon juice, strained

1 to 2 drops yellow food coloring

In the large bowl of an electric mixer, cream the butter until it is light and fluffy. Beat in the lemon zest and almond extract. Sift together the flour, powdered sugar, cornstarch and salt. Add the flour mixture to the creamed mixture and combine thoroughly.

Divide the dough into two equal portions. On a very lightly floured surface, roll each portion into a log 1½ to 1¾-inches in diameter. Wrap the logs in plastic wrap and refrigerate them until the dough is very cold and firm, at least 1 hour. (The dough may be kept for up to a week before it is baked.)

Preheat the oven to 350°F. Position the oven rack in the center of the oven.

Lightly grease one or two baking sheets. Using a serrated knife, slice each chilled log of dough into 16 to 18 slices, about ⅛-inch thick, and place about an inch apart on the baking sheet. Bake the cookies (one baking sheet at a time) about 8 to 10 minutes, watching carefully after 6 or 7 minutes of baking and, if necessary, rotating the pan to ensure even baking. The cookies are done when the edges are barely golden brown and the tops are firm to the touch. Transfer to wire racks to cool.

ICING

Mix the powdered sugar with 2 teaspoons of the lemon juice and the yellow food coloring, one drop at a time, in a small bowl. If it is too thick to brush onto the cookies, add as much as you need of the remaining ½ teaspoon of lemon juice to the icing. Using a pastry brush, brush a thin glaze of icing over each cookie. (If you don't have a brush, drizzle on a few drops of icing and spread in a smooth layer with a rubber spatula.) Let the cookies cool completely. When the icing is hard, pack them into a covered container with waxed paper or plastic wrap between the layers. Cover loosely and store at room temperature. They will keep for up to two weeks.

Makes 3 dozen 2½-inch cookies.

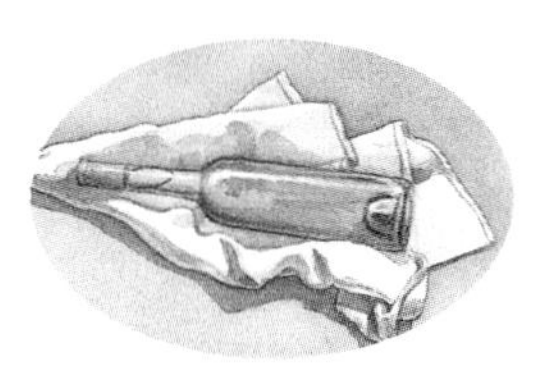

VIANSA WINE SUGGESTION
'Musecco' Muscat Canelli or 'Imbianco' Barbera Rosé

PASTICCINI CON ALBICOCCHE E PISTACCHI

Apricot Pistachio Pastry Rolls

CRUST

24 sheets filo dough (one 1-pound box), thawed

1 cup butter (2 sticks), melted

FILLING

1 cup shelled pistachios, lightly toasted and finely chopped

2 tablespoons brown sugar

¼ teaspoon ground ginger

1 teaspoon anise seed, crushed

¼ teaspoon cinnamon

Pinch of ground cloves

⅓ cup butter, melted

Grated zest of 1 lemon

2 cups dried apricots

1 cup fruity white wine (such as Viansa 'Musecco' Muscat Canelli)

APRICOT GLAZE

⅔ cup apricot jam

2 tablespoons finely chopped pistachios

CRUST

Brush each sheet of filo dough with butter. Fold it in half lengthwise, butter it and then fold it in half lengthwise again, so that you have a long rectangular sheet. Butter again.

FILLING

In a small bowl, combine the finely chopped pistachios, brown sugar, spices, butter and lemon zest and mix well. Heat the apricots and wine together in a covered saucepan on low heat until apricots are plump. Remove apricots and cool. Save wine for another use. Slice the apricots into thin slices.

Spread 2 teaspoons of the pistachio mixture on one end of each long filo rectangle. Top each rectangle with 6 to 8 strips of sliced apricot and roll up, forming a tube-like roll. Place rolls on a baking sheet, seam side down.

APRICOT GLAZE

Preheat oven to 350°F.

In a small saucepan, heat the apricot jam over very low heat until hot, about 3 minutes. Stir continuously, as it burns easily. When the jam is hot, press it through a strainer into a small bowl. Discard the chunks of apricot or save for another use. Keep the remaining syrupy part warm, carefully reheating if necessary. Brush or spoon 1 teaspoon glaze on top of each roll. Sprinkle ¼ teaspoon finely chopped pistachios on top of each roll. Bake for 20 minutes, until lightly browned. Serve hot or cold.

Makes 24 rolls.

Throughout the day all over Tuscany, visitors and locals alike pop into the multitude of cafes, bars, gelaterias, ristorantes, pizzerias and alementari (even gas stations!) for a quick cup of espresso, often accompanied by little pastries—or pasticcini—such as these.

VIANSA WINE SUGGESTION

'Athena' Dolcetto, 'Musecco' Muscat Canelli or 'Imbianco' Barbera Rosé

PASTICCINI RACCOLTA

Mini Harvest Cakes

When I created these little cakes for fall and winter in the Marketplace, I was concerned that they might be unpopular. But isn't California famous for its fruit and nuts? Isn't this the time of year when most people buy nuts and dried fruit? Yes, yes, I tried to convince myself. My fear, though, was that my delicious (and light!) little cakes might go the way of many holiday fruitcakes and end up as doorstops or in the garbage can.

Needless to say, I was relieved as they flew out the door in the hands of hungry or gift-minded visitors. In fact, they do have a long life (two weeks), and many of our visitors found them well-suited to the holidays!

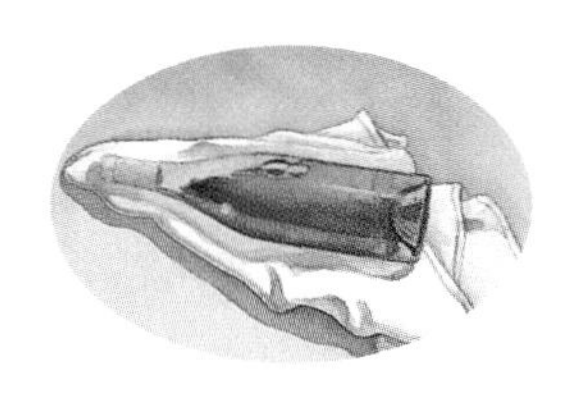

VIANSA WINE SUGGESTION

'Riserva Anatra Bianco' Trebbiano, Nebbiolo or Reserve Chardonnay

1 cup dried apricots

1 cup dates, pitted

1 cup dried apples

1 cup sun-dried Mission figs, stems removed (optional)

1 cup walnuts, broken into large pieces

1 cup hazelnuts

1 cup cashews

½ cup flour

¼ teaspoon salt

1 teaspoon baking powder

½ cup sugar

3 egg whites

3 egg yolks, well beaten

2 teaspoons Amaretto

Remove any pits or stems from the dried fruit and cut into ¾-inch pieces. Combine fruit and nuts in a large bowl. Combine flour, salt, baking powder and sugar in a small bowl and mix well. Pour dry ingredients over fruit and mix well.

Preheat oven to 325°F.

Beat egg whites until stiff but still moist. In a small bowl, beat the yolks with a whisk or fork until slightly foamy. Add Amaretto to egg yolks and whisk to combine. Carefully fold the yolks into the beaten egg whites. Then fold egg mixture into the fruit and nut mixture and mix gently but thoroughly.

Lightly grease 8 to 10 ramekins or custard cups (Pam spray works fine). A muffin tin can be substituted (it's much easier to remove the cakes and clean the tin if you use paper liners). Spoon the batter into the cups.

Bake at 325°F for 15 minutes, and then reduce heat to 300°F and bake for 20 minutes, until crust is golden brown (if using muffin tin or other thin-walled pan, reduce the second bake time to 15 minutes). Remove from the oven and cool for at least 30 minutes. To remove cakes from ramekins, run a knife around the edges. The Harvest Cakes will last up to two weeks wrapped tightly in plastic wrap and stored at room temperature.

Makes 8 to 10 small cakes if using ¾ cup ramekins or custard cups.
Makes 12 to 14 mini cakes if using muffin tin.

CROSTATA DI GORGONZOLA E MELE

Glazed Gorgonzola Apple Tart

CRUST
1 cup all-purpose flour

⅓ cup powdered sugar

½ cup cold unsalted butter (1 stick), cut into pieces

Pinch of salt

FILLING
1½ cups crumbled Gorgonzola cheese (12 ounces)

2 to 3 red or green apples or pears (about 1 pound)

GLAZE
⅔ cup apricot jam

CRUST

Preheat oven to 350°F.

Combine flour, sugar, butter and salt in a food processor and process until the dough forms a large ball (or mix dough using your usual pie crust method). Press dough to about ⅛-inch thickness on the bottom and up the sides of a 9-inch fluted tart, quiche or pie pan with sides ¾ to 1-inch high. Bake for 25 to 30 minutes, until light golden brown. Remove from oven and set aside.

FILLING

Place gorgonzola pieces on the warm crust. Place in oven for 5 minutes or so, just until cheese has slightly melted. Spread the cheese evenly over the crust.

Core and thinly slice the apples or pears, leaving the skin on. Arrange the slices decoratively over the cheese (overlapping the slices fan-style looks nice).

GLAZE

In a small saucepan, heat the apricot jam over very low heat until hot, about 3 minutes. Stir continuously, as it burns easily. When the jam is hot, press it through a strainer into a small bowl. Discard the chunks of apricot or save for another use. Keep the remaining syrupy part warm, carefully reheating if necessary. Brush or spoon over the apple or pear slices, coating well.

Serves 10 to 12.

Most of Italy's cheeses are produced in Northern Italy, as is this blue-veined cow's milk cheese—gorgonzola. Its layers are lightly layered to encourage the formation and growth of the tasty blue mold. It can be sweet, creamy and mild in its youth—called dolce —or fuller-flavored and sharper as it ages—called piccante.

Gorgonzola has been made and enjoyed in Italy for over 1,000 years and is certainly a popular staple in our kitchens. This versatile and delicious tart can be served as an hors d'oeuvre, an appetizer, or at a picnic or buffet.

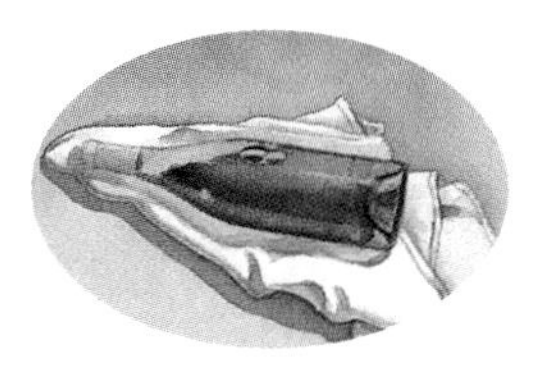

VIANSA WINE SUGGESTION
'Cento per Cento' Chardonnay, Reserve Chardonnay or 'Vittoria' Pinot Grigio

TIRAMISÙ SEDUCENTE

Tantalizing Tiramisù

This traditional and popular Italian dessert means, literally, "pick-me-up." It originated more than 20 years ago in Treviso, north of Venice in the Véneto region, and quickly became very popular, spawning many different versions.

It is made with espresso, rum, cocoa powder and rich Italian mascarpone cream cheese—an essential ingredient in Tiramisù. Many specialty food stores and gourmet supermarkets now carry mascarpone; it's worth seeking out.

8 ounces mascarpone cheese

5 tablespoons + 2 teaspoons sugar

5 teaspoons rum

6 egg yolks, beaten

1½ cups milk

3 egg whites

1 cup very strong, hot coffee (preferably 4 tablespoons instant espresso dissolved in 1 cup hot water)

1 package (7 ounces) ladyfingers

1 small (1.55 ounce) chocolate bar

1 teaspoon cocoa powder

In a medium-size bowl, stir together the mascarpone cheese, 1 tablespoon of the sugar and 2 teaspoons of the rum.

In a small saucepan, combine the egg yolks, 3 tablespoons sugar and the milk over medium-low heat. Cook for about 3 minutes, stirring constantly, until thick and hot. Watch carefully, as all of a sudden it thickens; don't overcook. Transfer to a mixing bowl and allow to cool. When egg custard is cool, add half of the mascarpone mixture and whisk well to thoroughly combine. Set aside.

Beat the egg whites in an electric mixer until soft peaks form. With the motor running on high, slowly add 2 teaspoons sugar. Continue beating until stiff peaks form. Fold the beaten egg whites into the remaining half of the mascarpone mixture and set aside.

In a shallow bowl, mix together coffee, the remaining tablespoon of sugar and 3 teaspoons of rum. Quickly dunk half of the ladyfingers (one at a time) into the coffee mixture and line the bottom of an 8x8-inch shallow serving dish. Spread the egg white and mascarpone mixture over the ladyfingers. With a vegetable peeler, peel the chocolate bar into shavings and sprinkle over the top of the egg white layer.

Arrange another layer of dunked ladyfingers on top and then spread the custard mixture over them.

Place the cocoa powder in a small strainer with very fine mesh; carefully tap the strainer to sprinkle the cocoa over the surface of the Tiramisu.

Chill for 1 to 2 hours before serving.

Serves 8.

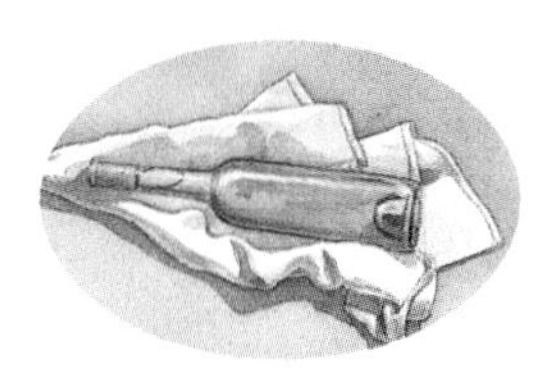

VIANSA WINE SUGGESTION
'Musecco' Muscat Canelli

PANNA COTTA DI CAFFÉ E COCCO

Coconut Coffee Mousse

¾ cup milk

1 envelope unflavored gelatin (about ¼ ounce)

⅔ cup sugar

¼ teaspoon salt

2½ tablespoons instant coffee powder (not freeze-dried)

2 cups whipping cream

1 cup shredded coconut, toasted

Pour milk into a small saucepan and sprinkle gelatin into it. Let stand for 5 minutes for gelatin to soften. Mix in sugar and salt. Heat, stirring until the gelatin, sugar and salt dissolve, about 5 minutes. Remove from heat and chill until slightly thickened (the consistency of egg whites), approximately 35 minutes.

Dissolve coffee powder in the whipping cream and beat until stiff. Thoroughly fold the whipped cream mixture and ⅔ cup of the toasted coconut into the gelatin mixture.

Spoon mixture into six individual dessert dishes or glasses and freeze for 1½ to 2 hours until firm (be careful not to freeze rock hard). If desired, freeze in a deep bowl or plastic freezer container, then scoop out with an ice cream scoop to serve. Slightly thaw if necessary; the consistency should be slightly soft and fluffy. Top frozen mousse with reserved toasted coconut.

NOTE: The coffee flavor is about medium strength. I love the taste of coffee in just about anything, but if you prefer a milder coffee flavor, reduce the amount in the recipe by a teaspoon or so.

Serves 6.

Panna Cotta refers to desserts made with cream or whipped cream, with many delicious regional variations. I designed this rich little mousse to be made quickly and to feature my favorite ingredients — coffee and coconut. One of my fondest memories of our family travels is my son Christopher's willingness to try any coconut dessert he could find up and down Italy—proving to me that coconut is, indeed, an Italian ingredient!

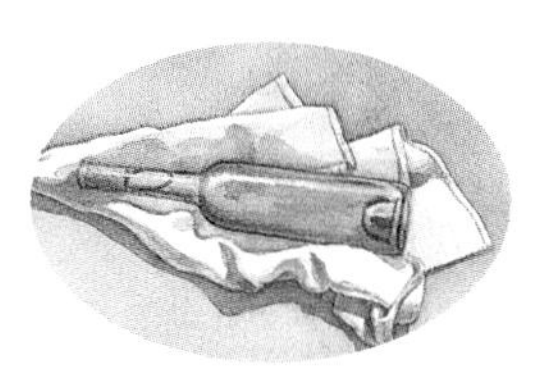

VIANSA WINE SUGGESTION
'Musecco' Muscat Canelli

SPECIALITA DALLA DISPENSA DI VIANSA

Specialties from Viansa's Pantry

CARAMEL SAUCE & RASPBERRY CHOCOLATE SAUCE

- Top peach halves with toasted pecans and drizzled sauce
- Sprinkle toasted pine nuts over rice pudding and drizzle with either sauce
- Drizzle melted sauce over butter sautéed peaches, pears, strawberries or bananas

FIGS IN SPICED WINE SYRUP

- Serve as a condiment with your holiday turkey or ham
- Wrap a slice of portobello mushroom and fig with bacon and sauté for hors d'oeuvres
- Mix diced figs, toasted pine nuts and cream cheese for a bagel or baguette spread

EXTRA VIRGIN OLIVE OIL

- Toss with cooked pasta to prevent sticking
- Brush on vegetables, meat or fish before grilling
- Serve with bread, instead of butter
- Toss with tuna, minced celery, cannellini beans and pepper for Italian antipasti
- Heat with minced garlic and salt for artichokes, crab or lobster dip
- Mix with crushed pink peppercorns and drizzle over salmon

VINEGARS

- Dissolve sugar in Balsamic Vinegar for a fruit marinade
- Blend Balsamic Vinegar with sour cream or yogurt for a tasty dip
- Drizzle Cabernet Vinegar over steamed chard and top with freshly grated Parmesan cheese
- Add a splash of Cabernet Vinegar to vegetable soups for added flavor
- Sauté minced shallots and Vinegar and add to salad dressings

PESTOS

- Stir into dressings to liven up pasta, rice, tuna, vegetable or green salads
- Add to omelets, pizza, frittatas or enchiladas for added flavor
- Stir into sour cream or yogurt as a topping for baked potatoes
- Stir into ground sirloin for great hamburgers
- Spread under loosened skin of chicken breasts prior to cooking
- Add to turkey stuffing
- Blend Olive Anchovy Pesto with mayo for a calamari dip
- Mix with butter for corn on the cob

RED PEPPER RELISH

- Serve with grilled lamb, roasted pork, country paté or chilled veal
- Mix with cream cheese and spread on baguette slices
- Spoon into mushroom caps and bake until browned
- Spoon a dollop on a baked potato or a deviled egg

SPECIALITA DALLA DISPENSA DI VIANSA

Specialties from Viansa's Pantry

MUSTARDS

- Try Hot Sweet Mustard with ham, Rosemary Mustard with lamb and Balsamic Country Mustard with poultry or fish
- Add a spoonful to olive oil, wine vinegar and minced fresh herbs for a salad dressing
- Blend Hot Sweet Mustard with olive oil, mayonnaise, minced garlic and basil for a cracked crab or artichoke dip
- Mix with marmalade to marinate and baste lamb
- Thin Hot Sweet Mustard with white wine and honey for a zesty chicken or game hen marinade
- Add to egg, tuna or potato salad for a zip
- Baste holiday ham or turkey with Hot Sweet Mustard and Balsamic Vinegar paste

TUSCAN COUNTRY VINAIGRETTE & CAESAR DRESSINGS

- Drizzle warm Vinaigrette over steamed green beans
- Mix Caesar with canned tuna and stuff a ripe tomato
- Blend cottage cheese, Caesar and a dash of white Worcestershire sauce for a tasty vegetable dip
- Sauté fresh spinach or chard in Vinaigrette and sprinkle with freshly grated parmesan
- Add Caesar to mayonnaise for potato salad
- Baste grilled steak or hamburgers with Vinaigrette

AIOLIS

- Spread on smoked turkey or trout sandwiches
- Use as a dip for artichoke leaves or asparagus
- Serve with crab cakes, cracked crab or fried calamari
- Combine with minced onion and spread on sea bass, catfish or salmon before broiling
- Spread on bread to make any sandwich a superstar

BLUE CHEESE BUTTER

- Spread on toast triangles that have been rubbed with garlic
- Toss with roasted potatoes or spoon over a baked potato
- Place a spoonful on top of any cooked vegetable, grilled meat or sautéed fish
- Warm and dip artichoke leaves, cracked crab or grilled prawns
- Add with thinly sliced apples to a melted cheese sandwich.

L'ABBINAMENTO DEI VINI VIANSA

Pairing Viansa Wines with Your Menu

'PICCOLO TOSCANO' ***Sangiovese***
- Risotto with prosciutto and mushrooms
- Pizza with peppers, olives and goat cheese
- Hearty minestrone
- Veal and pepper cannelloni
- Chocolate chip cookies

'DI PACOMIO' ***Aleatico***
- Raspberry basted ham
- Brie and apples
- Pecan pie
- Blueberry scones
- Poached salmon with strawberry salsa
- Young pecorino

'VITTORIA' ***Pinot Grigio***
- Grilled fennel and prawn skewers
- Boned tarragon game hen with celery-curry sauce
- Scallops with raspberry salsa
- Fontina cheese
- Crepes with smoked trout and toasted pine nuts

PRINDELO
- Herb crusted lamb chops
- Grilled portobello mushrooms
- Pasta with smoked ham and red peppers
- Osso bucco
- Pasta with porcini sauce

'ATHENA' ***Dolcetto***
- Blueberry cheesecake
- Goat cheese and toasted or smoked almonds
- Sweet potato tart
- Gravlox
- Fruitcake

NEBBIOLO
- Barbecued pork ribs with nectarine chutney
- Veal and fennel ravioli
- Sausage and sage stuffed turkey
- Scallops with raspberries and pecans
- Nebbiolo poached pears with creamed cinnamon mascarpone

'CENTO PER CENTO' ***Chardonnay***
- Lobster with garlic butter
- Salmon Ravioli with pine nuts and snow peas
- Oysters with basil and shallots
- Roasted chicken with Porcini and Prosciutto
- Crab cakes

'MUSECCO' ***Muscat Canelli***
- Prosciutto wrapped cantaloupe slices
- Tropical fruit salad with mint cream
- Apricot tart with toasted pecans
- Bread pudding

'IMBIANCO' ***Barbera Rosé***
- Spicy chicken pot stickers
- Paté and spiced figs
- Pork loin with peach chutney
- Picnics
- Provolone and Tallegio cheese
- Smoked ham with balsamic-berry sauce

'AUGUSTO' ***Barbera***
- Grilled Italian sausage
- Asiago cheese
- Liver and onions
- Beef tongue with sage sauce
- Biscotti

'OSSIDIANA' ***Cabernet Franc/Cabernet Sauvignon***
- Filet mignon with mushroom butter
- Smoked tomato and goat cheese tart
- Walnuts and cambozola cheese
- Cabernet-glazed pork tenderloin with chestnuts and juniper

'THALIA' ***Sangiovese***
- Veal parmesan
- Risotto with smoked chicken and eggplant
- Veal with wild mushrooms
- Grilled duck breast with cherry-orange chutney
- Tomato pasta with toasted pine nuts and sun-dried tomatoes

'RISERVA ANATRA BIANCO' ***Trebbiano***
- Twice baked potatoes with caramelized onions and fennel
- Herb roasted pheasant with apples, onions and sage
- Turkey with hazelnut and winter squash stuffing
- Grilled vegetables

'RISERVA ANATRA ROSSO' ***Cabernet Sauvignon***
- Braised or grilled venison
- Vintage cigars
- Eggplant parmesan
- Chilled lamb and gorgonzola salad with walnuts
- Garlic, herb and chili rubbed steaks

'REGALO DI CERTOSA' ***Grappa***
- Cigars
- Biscotti
- Espresso—"Café Correto"
- Fresh mint leaves

RESERVE CABERNET SAUVIGNON
- Rack of lamb with herb sauce
- Escargot
- Chocolate truffles
- Prime Rib with ricotta-horseradish sauce
- Wild boar paté with spiced figs

RESERVE CHARDONNAY
- Linguini with smoked salmon
- Risotto with pumpkin and pecans
- Pappardelle with basil pesto
- Baked chicken breast with walnuts and onions
- Roasted rabbit with polenta

CABERNET SAUVIGNON
- New York steak with green peppercorn sauce
- Risotto with smoked duck and walnuts
- Gourmet hamburger with gorgonzola
- Cabernet-cranberry marinated and braised lamb roast

CHARDONNAY
- Sea bass with basil sauce
- Fettuccine with Gorgonzola cream sauce
- Garlic and rosemary roasted chicken
- Risotto with prawns, sweet peppers and pine nuts
- Roasted herb potatoes

SAUVIGNON BLANC
- Smoked provolone and pecorino cheese
- Lemon chicken with shallots and Italian parsley
- Saffron risotto
- Steamed mussels with parsley and watercress
- Veal Piccata
- Caesar salad
- Pizza with artichokes and clams
- Frittatas

TUSCAN CLUB *The Premier Wine and Food Club of Viansa Winery*

I would like to introduce you to our Tuscan Club, a gourmet wine and food experience uniting the tradition and history of Italy with the excitement and innovation of California. Each month Tuscan Club members join Sam and me on a culinary tour of Tuscany as they receive a shipment of Viansa wine and specialty foods.

In Sam's monthly wine notes he shares the details of our Italian varietals, vineyard and cellar techniques and his winemaking secrets. Cucina members are the first to try my newest gourmet pantry foods from Viansa's Italian Marketplace and sample my culinary discoveries from Tuscany. Each month I create an exciting menu and special recipes—California fresh with an Italian influence!

Tuscan Club members immediately become VIPs at Viansa. They receive invitations to special winery dinners and events, access to private tours of the winery and wetlands and tastings in our exclusive Enoteca.

As one of our members put it: "Each month you bring my California heart into my East Coast body. With anticipation I look forward to the arrival of my Viansa 'surprise' package. It's been one of the nicest treats we could have given ourselves."

We invite you to share the California and Italian good life with us through one of four unique Tuscan Club plans:

VINO & CUCINA

Each shipment includes two bottles of Viansa wine specially selected by Sam, allowing you to sample the wide array of California and Italian varietals produced at Viansa. It also includes a collection of gourmet foods that I have created or selected. Sam and I write winemaker notes, chef notes, a seasonal menu and recipes and suggestions using the foods in the shipment.

SOLO VINO

Solo Vino members receive two bottles of Viansa wine and Sam's winemaker notes, along with information on the vineyards and wetlands.

Premio Memberships

PREMIO VINO & CUCINA

This plan is ideal for the wine and food connoisseur who desires a deluxe collection of premium and limited release wines along with the finest gourmet foods. Each month Sam selects a varying number of special wines from his cellar or private library, including seasonal new releases that are not yet available to the public. I choose an abundance of specialty foods beyond what the Vino & Cucina members receive, and create an additional menu and recipes to best enjoy these savory treats. Each shipment also includes Sam's winemaker notes and my chef notes.

PREMIO SOLO VINO

The choice for true wine aficionados, this plan includes a monthly shipment of special wines from Sam's cellar and private collection. The number and size of bottles varies from month to month as Sam chooses only the finest wines to share with Premio members. Each shipment also includes Sam's winemaker notes.

WE INVITE YOU TO JOIN US FOR VIANSA'S MONTHLY

"TASTE OF TUSCANY"

TUSCAN CLUB PRIVILEGI

One of the many special benefits available to Tuscan Club members is additional savings on all Viansa wines purchased at the winery or by mail.

	REGULAR DISCOUNT	TUSCAN CLUB MEMBER*
1 Case of wine	10%	15%
2 Cases of wine	15%	20%
4+ Cases of wine	15%	25%

**All case purchases are cumulative. Once four cases of Viansa wine have been purchased, all case purchases after that will qualify for the 25% discount.*

(Memberships may be cancelled after third order received.)

PLEASE CALL OR FAX US TODAY FOR CURRENT PRICES.

TOLL FREE NUMBER 1-800-995-4740 FAX 707-935-4731

25200 Arnold Drive, Sonoma, California 95476

INDICE

Index

INDICE

Index

INDICE

Index